WHAT YOU CAN BELIEVE ABOUT DRUGS

WHAT YOU CAN BELIEVE ABOUT DRUGS

An Honest and Unhysterical Guide for Teens

Susan and Daniel Cohen

M. Evans and Company, Inc.   New York

Library of Congress Cataloging-in-Publication Data

Cohen, Susan.

What you can believe about drugs.

Includes index.
1. Drugs.   2. Substance abuse.   3. Youth—Drug use.
I. Cohen, Daniel.   II. Title.
RM301.15.C63   1987   362.2'9   87-33160

ISBN 0-87131-527-0

M. Evans and Company, Inc.
216 East 49 Street
New York, New York 10017

Design by Dana Sloan
Manufactured in the United States of America
9 8 7 6 5 4 3 2

Contents

WHAT YOU CAN BELIEVE ABOUT DRUGS

1

A World
Like Ours

Pretend for a moment that this is a sci-fi story and you live on a distant planet. The time is now. The planet is a lot like Earth. And the country you live in looks very much like the United States of America. But there is a big difference. On this other planet cigarettes are banned and all tobacco products are illegal.

It's morning and you hurry to get dressed for school. Downstairs you find your mother—a former smoker in the days when cigarettes were still legal—busily stuffing her morning chewing gum in her mouth. Your mother never used to chew gum, but now to ward off her craving for tobacco she chews gum all the time. She's broken two teeth and her jaws ache constantly and she's gained twenty pounds because the gum doesn't keep her from eating like the cigarettes did. And she's always nervous and short-tempered. At least she's in better shape than your Aunt Mitzi who was caught at the airport smuggling in three cartons of cigarettes. Three trips to drug treatment centers have not cured your Aunt Mitzi of her nicotine addiction and so in a desperate attempt to find something to smoke she had gone on vacation to a country where tobacco is still grown openly. Now Aunt Mitzi is awaiting trial and her three cartons of cigarettes have been seized by the authorities. The family is hoping for a suspended sentence because this is her first offense.

You grab breakfast and meanwhile scan the newspaper en route to the sports page. The front-page headlines scream of a major gun battle between police and underworld cigarette dealers. Agents have been stationed at the borders of the country, stopping cars and searching for cigarettes. Also on the front page is a picture of a German Shepherd named Molly who's receiving a special award—Dog of the Year—thanks to her talent for sniffing out tobacco. She recently led her owner, an officer from the "Tobacco Squad," to a shed full of the stuff. The tobacco could not be burned for fear of drawing addicts to a deep breathe-in, so it had to be hauled away to be buried in a secret spot. On the front page there's an article that catches your eye. It describes the depression that's spread across regions of farmland which were once prosperous tobacco-growing districts. In protest the farmers have been holding demonstrations and blocking traffic on major highways.

It's time for you to leave for school. You pass the corner store, now closed and boarded up because it survived mainly on lottery tickets and cigarette sales. As you walk along you notice two people standing on the sidewalk melt into the shadows of a doorway. You know what's going on. An illegal cigarette deal. You glance cautiously at the pair as you pass them. It isn't safe to stare. The guy buying the cigarettes looks gaunt and filthy. His clothes are shabby. His sneakers are full of holes. Since it costs a hundred and fifty dollars for a pack of illegal cigarettes it's hardly surprising the smoker is desperately poor. Like a lot of addicts he probably has to steal to earn enough to support a two-pack-a-day habit. It's also scary to think about what he might be smoking. Cigarettes bought in the streets can be full of who knows what dangerous ingredients, and of course you never know how much or how little nicotine you're getting.

Of course, it isn't only the poor who smoke cigarettes. Bootleg cigarettes are everywhere. Although the number of police working on the tobacco squad is up and millions of dollars have been poured into fighting "the war on tobacco," the country is filled with secret smokers. You've heard rumors about expensive smoking clubs hidden in back of florist shops and restaurants in the rich parts of town where you have to know the right password to get in. The clubs are supposed to be very glamorous with everybody all dressed up, eager to show off their drug paraphernalia: silver cigarette cases and gold cigarette lighters. The clubs give out ashtrays to their best customers. Law enforcement officers in the pay of the tobacco kingpins look the other way and allow such clubs to flourish.

There are other kinds of clubs, too, dark and ugly where people just sit around and puff like crazy, getting high and listening to wild music. Sometimes there's a police raid and things turn violent. These kinds of clubs are located behind dry cleaning stores, bakeries, and video arcades.

No one in your family, not even your Aunt Mitzi (or so everyone fervently tries to believe) would go to a "smoke easy" like that. Yours is a law-abiding family. Well, it is true that your father has a small pile of pipe tobacco stashed away in the attic which you discovered snooping around after you'd been forbidden to go up there. Periodically your father finds some desperate excuse to vanish into the attic for a half hour or so.

Except for your father's occasional binges your family

have been model tobacco refusers. Including you. You've
hung anticigarette posters up in your bedroom. You're always first in line for a urine test where you invariably test
negative for nicotine. Alas, you do have one weakness. You
love old movies. Unfortunately, because of all the scenes
showing people smoking they've been banned. Sometimes
an uncontrollable urge comes over you to visit a friend
who's got a lot of Humphrey Bogart and Bette Davis movies,
and the two of you sit together in a darkened room fascinated by the sight of the smoke swirling around the heads
of the actors.

The sight of school looming up before you pulls you out
of your daydreams about old movies. You walk past the
knot of tough kids hanging around on the corner. The way
they dress makes grown-ups very angry. It could be the
earrings shaped like tobacco leaves or the leather cigarettes hanging from their belts. They wear buttons with the
familiar symbols "Camels," "Lucky Strike," and "Winston."
If you wanted tobacco the tough kids could get it for you,
but you're not looking for trouble so you enter the school.
The morning locker cigarettes search is finished so you're
free to go to class.

End of sci-fi story. Though it may seem farfetched or
even a little crazy, this story reveals a lot about the way
our society treats drugs today. Just substitute the word
marijuana or cocaine or heroin for cigarette and tobacco
in the story and see how differently it reads. In the story
there are two conflicting views of cigarettes. One group,
desperate to stamp them out, has become hysterical. This
group urges constant vigilance. It favors tough antismoking
laws, drug testing (for nicotine certainly is a drug), and
an all-out assault on tobacco and anyone who uses it.
The other group finds cigarettes romantic, exciting, and

14

glamorous. The more the respectable members of society tell them not to smoke, the more they're going to smoke.

Caught in the middle are the people who are addicted to nicotine and can't stop. They will commit any crime, pay any price to get their drug. Others, who aren't addicts and who generally obey most laws, enjoy an occasional cigarette, so they just go ahead and smoke once in a while hoping they don't get caught. Meanwhile in the midst of raids and drug busts, gangsters make a fortune peddling illegal cigarettes, and violence and corruption from this vast illegal market warp society.

But hey, wait a minute, maybe at this point you'd like to interrupt. Cigarettes are after all merely cigarettes, while cocaine, say, is dangerous. Cocaine can mess up your life. Cigarettes don't. Well, thanks for interrupting. It allows us to make a very important point about drugs and it is that legal drugs can be quite as dangerous as illegal drugs. Every society has drugs of choice which it tends to treat as non-drugs. There are historical reasons for these choices. Good sense had little to do with it.

Drugs of Choice

In America the three drugs of choice are alcohol, tobacco, and caffeine. In this book we will not be taking a close look at alcohol. For that see our *A Six-Pack and a Fake I.D.* As to caffeine, it's so much a part of our lives we hardly think about it, but just ask the average person to try to get through the day without a cup of coffee. Yet when is the last time you've heard someone referred to as "coffee-dependent," a "coffee abuser," or addicted to the stimulant caffeine? We'll touch more on caffeine later. For now let's get back to the more interesting subject of cigarettes.

Now cigarettes are highly dangerous. You know they've been linked to cancer of the lungs, heart disease, etc. Smoking kills more people than cocaine, heroin, and all the other illegal drugs combined. Cigarettes are also highly addictive—as addictive as cocaine or heroin, or worse, according to some experts. Despite well-publicized evidence of the dangers of smoking and one massive kick-the-habit campaign after another, a lot of people simply cannot stop smoking, or if they do stop temporarily go back to it. What's more it's almost impossible to limit cigarette smoking to one or two cigarettes a day, not if you inhale. One moves very quickly from being a beginning smoker to requiring a pack or more a day. Add to this that cigarettes stain your teeth, make your breath smell horrible, taste awful, and make you dizzy till you get used to them, and you can see that cigarettes are a potent, gruesome drug.

Many nonsmokers do strongly disapprove of cigarettes, and there are laws governing where people can smoke, but there is little public hysteria surrounding the issue of smoking. The subject is debated calmly. You may never meet a heroin addict, but you certainly know someone who smokes and assuredly someone who's addicted to nicotine. You've either tried cigarettes yourself or thought about trying them. You've heard a lot of facts but probably not too many lies about cigarettes, and even though a lot of kids smoke because smoking makes them feel grown up, cigarettes are much less mysterious and fascinating than illegal drugs.

In this book we're going to talk about illegal drugs in the same calm tone people generally use when they talk about cigarettes. We will not try to scare you or lie to you. For example, if we were to tell you as some antidrug brochures do that one marijuana cigarette will start you on the road to heroin addiction and a life of crime you'd probably laugh at us. And you would be right. If all the people in this society who've tried marijuana had become addicts and criminals society wouldn't function at all. You probably know someone who smokes marijuana from time to time or who's tried it: If the statistics on teenage marijuana use are right there is a good chance that you're the occasional pot smoker. But it hasn't turned you into a raging dope fiend or rotted your brain, and if we lied to you about marijuana or any other drug you'd come in contact with you wouldn't believe anything else we told you.

We will talk about the hysteria that surrounds drugs, of course, particularly when we get into the history of drugs and drugs in different cultures. We'll talk about specific drugs, too, and about the romance that surrounds them. But just as we don't intend to scare you we think you should know from the start that we don't find drugs mysterious or supernaturally irresistible. We're not impressed by the claims of those who feel drugs make you better or smarter or sexier than non-drug-users or that using drugs brings you to deeper insights into life.

We're also going to talk about those drugs that are supposed to make you look good, rather than feel good. These are the steroids and the diet pills, which are becoming a bigger part of the teenage scene.

We're going to try to tell it to you straight. No moralizing, no scare tactics, no romance. You're going to make the decisions. You're going to need the information.

Now, while we're at it let's try to define the word "drug." It's not as easy as you think. How about a substance or chemical that causes changes in the body or mind? But this definition could apply to foods, salt, even poison. "Psychoactive drugs," that is, drugs that affect the mind, at least seems to differentiate between drugs used for medical treatment and drugs used to achieve a high or to relax. But some drugs have been used both for medical treatment and to alter your state of consciousness. Drugs cannot simply be put in a good or bad category. Remember the old story—practically school folklore—about getting a cheap thrill by putting an aspirin in a glass of soda. Does that make aspirin a psychoactive drug?

As we said, it's not even easy to define the word "drug."

2

Teen Drug Stories

When we were growing up, we didn't take drugs. That's not meant to be a proclamation of superior morality. It's a simple statement of fact. We didn't know anyone who took drugs and even if we had wanted drugs we had no idea where to get them. Of course we drank, excessively and illegally. So did practically everyone else we knew. No one considered alcohol a drug. And we smoked—that was illegal, too, for teenagers. We heard it would "stunt our growth." We didn't know it might result in lung cancer thirty years later. Our parents worried about us a lot. Some of the worry was clearly justified.

When we were quite young there were some loopholes in the narcotics laws, and some opiates were still available in over-the-counter medicines. One was called paregoric. It was used to control diarrhea—very effectively, too. But we couldn't imagine anyone getting hooked on paregoric —it tasted awful, and the long-term effects—well, you can imagine. There were also cough medicines with another mild opiate, codeine. But these drugs were associated with illness—not getting high.

We had read—usually in fiction—of opium dens. Once in a while the newspapers carried a scary story about marijuana use among Mexican-Americans. Most of the time we heard about drugs in grim warnings passed out in school or intoned over the radio from the Federal Bureau of Narcotics. We were being warned about drugs we'd never even heard of—the warnings as we recall were more intriguing than frightening.

During the sixties, when many of our contemporaries were smoking a little pot or dropping a little acid, we remained firmly and obstinately part of the gin-and-beer generation. Later our daughter would bring back occasional tales of drug use in her high school. But these seemed like messages from a distant world—faint and difficult to understand.

When we sat down to put this book together we knew that one of the first things that we would have to do would be to try to get some feel of what drug use is like among teens of the late 1980s.

The "official" publications, that is most books and other material put out for teens today, present a picture of teenage drug use as an unrelieved scene of degradation and horror. This picture we knew to be badly distorted because we met too many bright, happy, and completely together pot smokers.

Often statistics about drug use are trotted out to terrify parents and other voters. There is a lot of pointing with alarm to figures like over half the kids in America have tried marijuana by the time they are eighteen, or sixteen percent have tried cocaine. But what do such statistics mean? The kid who smokes an occasional joint at a party or even snorts some cocaine is not the problem. Sure, by smoking or snorting he or she is doing something illegal. But in most states today drinking alcohol before you are twenty-one and driving above the speed limit are also illegal —and both of these activities can be dangerous as well.

The real problem is the kid who becomes dependent on a drug, either physically or psychologically. There may be other medical problems down the road, even for the occasional user, but the immediate problem is the dependency. Sure, if you never try any drug you will never become dependent on it. If everyone "just said no" as the slogan goes the drug problem would disappear entirely. But we live in America of the 1980s, not in the land of Oz (indeed there may even have been opium poppies in the land of Oz as well).

Anyone with the slightest knowledge of the history of drug use in America is going to realize that in one form or another drugs have been with us a long time. They are not going to be wished or willed away.

The kids that we talked to were mainly middle-class and middle-American. The story of the heroin addict who winds up hustling in Times Square is real enough. But it has been told often enough too. It's not the kind of life that most of you can relate to. Pretending that if you do a little cocaine that's how you're going to wind up may please some anti-drug crusaders. But you're not going to believe a word of it.

What follows are three accounts of teens who became more than casual drug users. Perhaps some of what you read will sound familiar to you—remind you of someone you know—perhaps you may even recognize a little of your own life.

Robin's Story

At sixteen Robin ran away from home, but then she'd never found home a very happy place. She'd grown up in a dreary New England manufacturing city where the factories were closing and there didn't seem to be much future in staying. Her parents divorced when she was three. Her mother was an alcoholic who vanished for long stretches of time. Her father moved to Texas where he remarried and had several children. Robin visited him a couple of times but always felt like the stranger in the family. There didn't seem to be any room for her in her father's new life.

Whenever her mother vanished Robin would go live with one or another of her mother's relatives. When her mother returned there would be a tearful reunion and promises that this time things would be different. But things weren't different. Her mother always started drinking again.

By the time Robin was a junior in high school she was too depressed to concentrate on her studies. Being in school was like being in prison. Her marks plummeted. She was on the outs with the popular kids. Robin's friends were the outcasts of the high school. They identified themselves by their music, their clothes, and their hair. Sometimes they took drugs. To the world at large they were obnoxious rebels, but they depended on one another. Robin's boyfriend, who had quit school, sold drugs from time to time to pick up spending money. He was good-looking and lots of fun. The day he abandoned Robin for another girl was the day Robin ran away from home.

Robin arrived at New York City's Port Authority Bus Terminal with only a few dollars in her pocket. The city seemed huge and intimidating but she had met a couple of people who lived in New York through her ex-boyfriend. They sold drugs, too. When Robin called them they said she could stay with them.

It isn't easy to find a home or a job when you're a sixteen-year-old runaway. The "drug culture" became Robin's home. Drug users (and abusers) helped her hide from the police, who are always on the lookout for runaways, by moving her from one apartment to another.

As she roamed around New York Robin met people she considered totally outrageous. Some were crazy. She liked the way they let their weirdness show. The drug culture seemed very glamorous. The people back home were tame and dull in comparison.

The drug users Robin knew helped her find work. One got her a false I.D. Another got her a job in a record store for a while. Robin made friends with a drug user who owned a jewelry store. When there was no work Robin begged for money in the streets and she usually got enough to buy food and marijuana and pay her subway fare to the next apartment.

Then Robin met Michael. He had dropped out of college and was drifting along the fringes of the drug world just as she was. She moved into an apartment with Michael in Brooklyn. Michael had been through the same things Robin had been through. His parents were divorced and his father was an alcoholic. Michael didn't know what he wanted to be in life or what he wanted to do. Neither did Robin.

There were some wonderful aspects to life with Michael. Robin came to share Michael's interest in music and books. The two spent hours talking about the past and wistfully wondering about the future.

But their lives still revolved around drugs. They couldn't imagine knowing people who didn't take them. They gave parties where everybody experimented with drugs (especially cocaine, which Robin considered a "conversation" drug) and discussed life and theories about life with great intensity.

Still, there were long boring afternoons when time passed with agonizing slowness because there were no drugs. And there was the night a really violent guy showed up at the apartment, and threatened to kill them both. He was looking for drugs and someone had given him Robin and Michael's address. Luckily he left without hurting anybody, but it was a scary moment.

Then Michael was nearly arrested buying drugs uptown and later was nearly arrested selling drugs downtown. The very thought of Michael in jail put Robin in a panic. She began to worry about other people she knew who were winding up in jail because of drugs or who were moving rapidly from heavy drug use to addiction. The idea that drugs were glamorous was wearing thin.

Robin is now eighteen and a student at Brooklyn College. Michael works at a bookstore in Manhattan. They're still together and they're both off drugs. There was no sudden dramatic moment when they built a bonfire and burned all their drugs or tossed them out the window.

Call it change, call it maturity, call it growing up. They got tired of drugs. They moved on to other things.

Andy's Story

Andy lived in a deeply conservative, small Midwestern town where his father was mayor. The town expected its mayor to be a model citizen. The mayor's children were expected to be ultra-good and ultra-obedient. For the first seventeen years of his life Andy succeeded in living up to his parents' standards. He studied hard at school, attended church faithfully every week, and sang in the church choir. He babysat regularly for his younger brothers and sisters, was consistently polite to his parents, and spent Saturday nights at home.

At seventeen he rebelled. Andy took a close look at the members of his family and decided they presented a false image to the world. It seemed to Andy that his father was an ambitious person who cared more about his potential political career than about his wife and children. Andy felt it was time to stop pretending to be perfect. The town could think what it liked. He, Andy, was going to show them the real Andy.

He stopped studying and started skipping classes. When his parents found out they were furious. Andy tried to talk to them, tried to explain what was going on inside him but they wouldn't listen. Fuming, Andy went to a party and smoked a joint. Marijuana seemed better than beer, so he went to the local pot party every Saturday night.

One night the cops caught him smoking marijuana. The chief of police told his father, who accused Andy of trying to ruin his political career. Andy's mother burst into tears. After that things at home went spiraling downward.

Andy's parents searched his room daily for drugs. He hid them at a friend's house. His parents nagged him endlessly about his falling marks. He yelled back. They ordered him to get counseling from the minister or a therapist. He wouldn't.

He began playing practical jokes on people. He spray-painted obscenities on the school wall when the football team lost. He and a friend stole a stop sign from in front of the police station. Andy phoned in false alarms to the volunteer fire fighters.

The whole town was asking pointed questions about Andy's upbringing so Andy's parents decided to ship him off to relatives in Florida. Andy was ready to go.

In Florida Andy met Wendy. Her parents were wealthy competitive people who liked to excel at everything they tried. Wendy's brother and sister were the same. Wendy felt estranged from her family because she was so unlike them. What was clear to them was foggy to her. She didn't like to compete. She had no specific goals. Though her parents wouldn't admit it, she knew they were disappointed in her.

Andy and Wendy turned eighteen just before they graduated from high school. Andy wondered whether he should join the army. Wendy wondered whether she should go to college. Instead, they hung around Wendy's house smoking marijuana and listening to music. After Wendy had an especially ghastly fight with her parents she climbed into her Saab, withdrew some money from her bank account, and with Andy in tow drove off to visit friends she knew in various parts of the country.

Everywhere it was the same. Andy and Wendy would show up at somebody's house and proceed to lie around all day smoking pot. They couldn't mobilize themselves to wash dishes or run a vacuum cleaner. Though they promised to get jobs they never did. The people they visited invariably grew weary and angry and finally threw them out.

Andy and Wendy are still traveling. Though they don't always appear unhappy and depressed they are unhappy and depressed. And they are bored. Drugs give them something to do and something to think about. Drugs provide a break in a basically dull routine.

They don't think drugs are the greatest thing in the world. They just can't imagine their lives without the drugs.

Ethan's Story

Ethan, 17, was a whiz in school. Bright, articulate, good in every subject, he was at the top of his class at a very classy high school in a wealthy New York suburb. Ethan prided himself on scoring in the 1300s on the SATs without really trying.

Ethan's social life was something else again. He wasn't an outcast. In his school people who achieved academically were respected. But he wasn't popular either. His interests ran to computers and science fiction, which he suspected made him seem kind of a nerd. He wasn't very muscular, he had acne and a big nose. He was convinced that was why girls didn't seem to want to go out with him.

Secretly Ethan dreamed of being bold, exciting, romantic, and popular. But even when he wore his hair in a modified mohawk one summer he looked rather ordinary. He was deeply afraid that he was essentially drab and colorless and that life would always be dull.

Actually Ethan was a lot more interesting than he realized, but part of the problem was his parents. They'd been hippies in the sixties and from the time he was small they'd filled his ears with tales of their youthful adventures. They smoked pot and took acid. They caroused their way through Europe and India, sleeping under the stars and begging for money when they were broke. They were arrested for swimming nude at a crowded public beach. Finally, they gave up all their material possessions and moved to a religious commune, shaved their heads, became vegetarians, and converted to Buddhism.

That was twenty years ago. Now Ethan's father worked on Wall Street and his mother was creative director at a small but very successful advertising agency. Ethan lived with his parents and younger sister in a large house with a swimming pool, a tennis court, and a Porsche and Mercedes in the garage. But Ethan's parents still loved to reminisce about the good old days when they were young rebels and every now and then they would still smoke pot.

Ethan romanticized the sixties. When he smoked pot or took LSD he felt fascinatingly different, extraordinary, a throwback to a more exciting era. Taking drugs also paid off for Ethan socially. He acquired a certain notoriety at school when he started using cocaine. People who otherwise would never have noticed him or would simply have considered him the kid who always got *A*'s in physics suddenly admired him.

Soon people were asking him to get them drugs. Ethan agreed, boasting of his "good connections." Buying drugs was an adventure in itself. It raised him above the common nerd herd at school. Selling drugs was even more prestigious. The danger of risking expulsion from school if he were caught selling drugs was especially intriguing. If it happened it wouldn't be quite as dramatic as being arrested for swimming nude at a public beach but it would sure be the talk of the dinner table.

Of course, Ethan wasn't quite what he pretended to be. He talked about drugs more than he took them, sold them only occasionally and very cautiously. His druggie pose made him a lot like the boy who parties once in a while but who tells everybody he'd drunk every night.

Ethan wasn't caught and he wasn't thrown out of school. He continued getting good marks and was accepted at a prestigious college. Drugs didn't turn him into a sixties-type hero. Drugs didn't bring him any girlfriends either. The one girl who liked him got tired of listening to him brag about his drug use and started going out with somebody else.

3

Narcotics— The Real Hard Drugs

In the movie *The Wizard of Oz,* Dorothy, Toto, the Scarecrow, the Cowardly Lion, and the Tin Woodman come upon a meadow of beautiful yellow poppies. These are no ordinary flowers. They put people into a deep sleep. In L. Frank Baum's original novel the poppies are a vivid scarlet and their scent makes people fall asleep forever. Perhaps Baum had the opium poppy in mind when he created these magic flowers. When *The Wizard of Oz* was published in 1900, America was a land filled with opium users and abusers. Painkillers containing drugs derived from opium were easy to buy. Just walk down to your neighborhood pharmacy or grocery store.

Opium and its derivatives don't automatically put people to sleep. But since opium puts some people into a dreamlike state it is traditionally associated with passivity and stupor. The Greek word for stupor is *narcotic,* and not accidentally opium and drugs derived from opium are lumped under the heading "narcotics." Morphine, the major active ingredient in opium, was named for Morpheus, the Greek god of dreams. Drugs derived from morphine and other opium compounds are called *opiates*.

Perhaps it's partly the link to dreams and sleep that gives narcotics their incredibly mysterious and sinister reputation. Listen to this description of an opium den (a place rather like a bar, only instead of alcohol, opium was sold there) in the Sherlock Holmes story "The Man with the Twisted Lip." Holmes's friend Dr. Watson tells of going through "a vile alley" near London Bridge. He goes down a flight of steps "leading to a black gap like the mouth of a cave." He enters a "long, low room, thick and heavy with the brown opium smoke and terraced with wooden berths like the forecastle of an emigrant ship." Bodies lie in "strange fantastic poses" and "out of the black shadows there glimmered little red circles of light, now bright, now faint, as the burning poison waxed or waned in the bowls of the metal pipes." Later, many a silent movie would incorporate this vision of the evil opium den with its "burning poison" and "torpid addicts."

It would be nice if we could tell you that the real reason opium was considered dangerous (when used for fun instead of as a medicine) was that it's so highly addictive. Addictive it is but that isn't the main reason. Unfortunately, as much as anything else it was prejudice that gave opium a bad name.

Opium was widely used in China. In the United States in the 1850s and 1860s thousands of Chinese men arrived on the West Coast to help build the Western railroad. Many smoked opium. A lot of people considered these new immigrants alien and mysterious. Therefore, the drugs the Chinese used had to be alien and mysterious too, unlike good old American booze. Most of the Chinese immigrants were poor, so the "dens" they established were by and large shabby places which only made their reputation worse. But even the existence of some rather posh opium dens in China and some large, reasonably comfortable opium dens in America couldn't soften the image. The general public considered saloons merely rowdy. Opium dens were sinister.

Then there's heroin. Heroin is an opiate, and no drug has a worse reputation. Made by heating morphine and acetic acid (which is found in vinegar), heroin is the drug non-users associate most with addiction, violent crime, and danger. So between opium dens and heroin addicts, narcotics have been stigmatized as something negative, something horrible. But from a medical standpoint narcotics are a boon to mankind.

When Karl Marx spoke of religion as "the opiate of the people" (a very unflattering phrase), in a sense he was paying homage to the position opium holds in the pantheon of drugs. After all, he didn't talk about "the cocaine of the people." The word opiate had made its way into common everyday language because opiates were a common everyday part of life.

Despite the image of the drowsy opium user opium does not automatically make people feel passive, gloomy, or down. Though narcotics are classified as depressants, so is alcohol, and you know yourself that people sometimes become aggressive and even violent when they drink too much. Narcotics make some users restless and anxious.

From Pleasure to Addiction

Narcotics are classified as depressants not because of the way they affect people's moods but because of the way they affect the central nervous system. Scientists don't really know why it is that in low doses depressants make people feel good. One theory holds that depressants act first on parts of the brain that make us feel sad or unhappy. By slowing down those parts of the brain depressants actually make us feel cheerful. Many people enjoy having a drink or two because alcohol relaxes them. In reasonable doses some people find narcotics enjoyable, too. The problem is that narcotics are extremely addictive. Sure, alcohol is an addictive drug, but it generally takes years to get hooked on alcohol. Narcotics turn users into addicts fast.

We owe our very conception of addiction (craving, tolerance, and withdrawal) to narcotics. We wish we could give you a blow-by-blow, detailed description of the addictive process and answer all your questions. But addiction is a very complicated subject and a lot is still unknown. Scientists can't even tell us if drug abuse causes permanent chemical changes in the body, changes which might explain why it's so hard to shake off a drug habit and stay clean.

Craving is an emotionally loaded word. It's meant to describe the overpowering need an addict feels for drugs. Once hooked on drugs addicts develop a tolerance to many of the drug's effects. This means that as time passes addicts get less pleasure from drugs than they once did but they can (even must) take higher doses without getting sick. Addicts can comfortably handle doses of drugs which would kill the occasional user or make him or her miserably ill.

When we say an addict needs drugs we're not kidding. Lack of drugs leads to withdrawal symptoms. When a narcotics addict stops taking drugs he or she experiences sweating, nausea, weakness, headache, restlessness, and/ or increased sensitivity to pain.

Obviously withdrawal from narcotics is at the very least highly unpleasant and often it can be downright horrible.

But withdrawal rarely proves fatal. Actually withdrawal from alcohol can be quite as ghastly or even worse than withdrawal from narcotics and in extreme cases it's more dangerous. But arguing about whether withdrawal from alcohol is better or worse than withdrawal from narcotics is like arguing over whether it's better to be hit by a truck than a bus. Who cares?

One of the most treacherous aspects of addiction is that it is extremely hard to cure. Even after a narcotics addict's body is drug-free and he's technically cured he may still be addicted. The rate of relapse among so-called cured narcotics addicts is depressingly high. Some people spend their whole lives in a cycle of addiction, imprisonment followed by treatment followed by addiction, followed by imprisonment, etc.

After all this grisly information you may think we were crazy describing narcotics as a boon to mankind a few pages back. Well, if you've ever been really sick or in pain and a doctor prescribed codeine (among other things good for suppressing coughs) or Demerol (a synthetic opiate and strong pain reliever) for you then you know what relief narcotics used wisely can provide. You can see why opium poppies were widely prized plants even thousands of years ago.

Opium comes from the green pods of the poppy which begin to ripen as the flowers of the plant start to wither. If the pods ripen fully they turn brown and dry and the seeds they contain can be gathered and used in cooking. But if the pods are slashed open before they ripen they ooze a milky juice. This juice when dried is crude opium. Originally opium poppies probably grew only in southern Europe and western Asia but now the poppy is cultivated in many parts of the world. Crude opium contains many drugs and tastes perfectly awful.

Morphine and Needles

Opium and the drugs derived from it can cause nausea, vomiting, dizziness, and constipation. They make the pupils of the eyes contract, often to pinpoints.

Medicine took a major leap forward (and alas so did drug addiction) when morphine was extracted from opium in the early nineteenth century and the hypodermic syringe was invented in the 1850s. This meant that morphine, a highly potent, highly addictive drug in white powder form, could be mixed with water and injected directly into someone's body in large fast-acting doses. Injections of morphine can kill the pain caused by an injury or operation very effectively.

But a massive dose of narcotics can also kill by depressing the respiratory system to the point where the victim of the overdose stops breathing. In the late nineteenth century chemists experimenting with morphine produced heroin. Heroin is very similar to morphine but is even more potent. (For a brief period heroin was considered a miracle cure for morphine addiction.) Morphine, heroin, and the hypodermic syringe! The age of modern superdrugs had arrived. But America had already overdosed on drugs.

In the nineteenth century America experienced an absolute explosion of drug use. Drugs were given to teething babies, to men who had been disabled in the Civil War, to middle-aged women for what was discreetly labeled "women's complaints," often menopausal symptoms. Drugs were given to grieving widows to help them feel less unhappy. Narcotics could even be ordered by mail. Patent medicines with opium or morphine had names like *Mrs. Winslow's Soothing Syrup, Glyco-Heroin Compound,* and *McMunn's Elixir of Opium.* These nonprescription drugs were widely marketed and heavily advertised. Clever salesmen boasted that drugs were the hottest items around.

As for drug addicts they were everywhere. Some were women who stayed home and visited the medicine cabinet while their husbands went off to visit the neighborhood saloon. Some, male and female alike, were members of strong prohibitionist antialcohol church groups who wouldn't dare drink whiskey but who didn't hesitate to gulp down drugs. Many users were people who had become addicted to drugs in hospitals where excessive amounts of narcotics were routinely given to ease pain.

The playwright Eugene O'Neill's mother became addicted accidentally when a doctor prescribed drugs for her during an illness. O'Neill wrote a harrowing play about the tragic results of her addiction called *A Long Day's Journey into Night*. However, addiction wasn't always disastrous. Many addicts lived normal lives in the nineteenth century. Because drugs were legal, cheap, and easily obtained, addicts weren't driven to crime to support their habits. They married, held jobs, owned businesses, remained with their families, went to school, and went to church. Addiction wasn't approved of any more than alcoholism is approved of now but it didn't make you an outcast or bring the cops to your door. It didn't necessarily shorten your life span either.

Thomas De Quincey, who was born in the late eighteenth century, became an opium addict as a young man. He remained addicted all his life and lived to the ripe old age of seventy-four. When De Quincey was in his late thirties he wrote a book called *Confessions of an English Opium Eater*, which made him a celebrity. Actually the book should have been called *Confessions of an English Opium Drinker*, since De Quincey drank opium in a concentrated form called laudanum which you add to water. He began drinking laudanum because he had a bad toothache. Medicine and dentistry were still quite primitive in De Quincey's time and there wasn't much you could do to relieve the pain and suffering disease caused except take opium or alcohol. A hundred drops of laudanum a day was a high but not extraordinary pain-killing dosage. De Quincey's laudanum habit reached several thousand drops a day but he kept right on living life as usual and writing.

The English poet Samuel Taylor Coleridge, who wrote "The Rime of the Ancient Mariner" and "Kubla Khan," praised the tranquilizing effects of laudanum. Some experts believe the way the drug affected Coleridge influenced him in his work, contributing to the exotic style of his poetry. Coleridge certainly was an addict. He sometimes guzzled two quarts of laudanum a week! This was a giant-sized habit.

The Strange Case of Dr. Halsted

Then there was Dr. William Stewart Halsted, who "cured" his cocaine habit by becoming a morphine addict. This prominent American surgeon was born into a prestigious New York family in the 1850s. He was a man who had everything going for him, becoming captain of the Yale football team in college and achieving success as a doctor while he was still in his twenties.

How did the eminent Dr. Halsted become a cocaine addict in the first place? It happened in the most innocent way. While testing cocaine to see if such a thing as a local anesthetic that would deaden pain could be developed Dr. Halsted injected himself repeatedly with the drug. Though his findings proved a real breakthrough he became so badly addicted he couldn't continue his medical career.

Dr. Halsted tried several times to kick the cocaine habit but couldn't. Then he spent several months in a hospital and this time when he emerged he was finished with cocaine. Held up to the world as an example of moral strength, he was viewed as a man of noble character who had fought the battle against drugs and triumphed. Dr. Halsted went on to help found the great Johns Hopkins Hospital, becoming chief of surgery there. He worked hard for years. His health was good. He married, living happily with his wife for thirty-two years. If this isn't a success story, what is?

It wasn't until 1969 that the truth about Dr. Halsted came out. He hadn't cured his addiction. He had simply traded one form of addiction for another. Interestingly, though Dr. Halsted couldn't function well as a cocaine addict he functioned extremely well as a narcotics addict, and remained a narcotics addict until his death.

Dr. Halsted's story is very revealing because though we like to think we're much more sophisticated and worldly than people were in Dr. Halsted's era we still tend to view drug addiction in moralistic terms today. Addicts are seen as people too weak or evil to overcome their need for drugs. Addicts who struggle against their addiction and free themselves from drugs are perceived as strong and good. Addicts who stubbornly continue taking drugs are perceived as weak failures. Dr. Halsted had to keep his drug addiction a secret or he would have been denounced as weak or worse.

Was Dr. Halsted weak? Are the teenagers and adults you know who smoke cigarettes weak, stubborn, or "bad" because they can't give up tobacco? We know far too little about addiction to jump to conclusions about why some people remain addicted and others don't. If anything Dr. Halsted's addiction proves that strong smart people can become just as solidly hooked on drugs as weak dumb people.

But wait a minute. Doesn't Dr. Halsted's story prove that narcotics should be legalized and made available to addicts at a low price? If Dr. Halsted hadn't been able to get the morphine he needed legally then instead of being one of

America's foremost doctors he might have become one of America's foremost criminals, forced to do anything to get hold of drugs. Just distribute drugs to addicts and there would be no drug problem.

Unfortunately, things aren't that simple. Look at alcohol. Anybody who really wants a drink can find one. Yet our society is awash in problems brought on by alcohol even though it's a legal drug. And what about prescription drugs legally obtained? Diet pills, sleeping pills, and tranquilizers have caused a lot of problems. Just because a drug is labeled socially acceptable doesn't mean it won't be abused.

As for Dr. Halsted, he didn't become an addict because he was trying to escape from stress, cheer himself up, or have more fun at parties. People who seek drugs out because they are bored, depressed, and unhappy may buy temporary relief from their problems, but ultimately the problems will return to plague them. Dr. Halsted led a productive, satisfying life as an addict because he'd led a productive, satisfying life before. Many addicts nowadays are in trouble even before they try drugs. Supplying addicts with drugs may or may not be a good idea (we'll go into the arguments pro and con on this elsewhere) but it would not be a magic solution.

In the early twentieth century the government began requiring doctors to keep records of prescriptions and manufacturers of patent medicines were ordered to limit the amounts of opium in their products. The public was beginning to take drug addiction seriously. Still, morphine and heroin were perceived as safer and, strange as it may sound, more genteel than alcohol. People looked around and saw that narcotics addicts remained reasonably healthy while alcoholics often developed a constellation of diseases including cirrhosis of the liver, which is fatal. Nonusers noticed that many narcotics addicts were middle-class.

Though drugs were hardly unknown to the poor, the image of the drunken bum sprawled on the sidewalk unable to hold a job made people associate alcohol with poverty. In England gin was seen as the scourge of the slums.

Today heroin has become our gin, the scourge of our slums. When poor people become addicted they must get money for drugs any way they can including robbery. Even the word *heroin* conveys the image of a robber mugging someone in the streets. The stigma attached to heroin in our society is so great it's forbidden even as a painkiller. You may be given a shot of morphine in an American hospital after surgery but you won't be given a shot of heroin.

Over the past two decades heroin use has spread to the middle class. Some affluent teenagers play around with heroin by injecting it under the skin or sniffing (snorting) it. Either method is less likely to lead to addiction than injecting heroin directly into a vein. Others try to avoid addiction by injecting themselves intravenously only occasionally, say before a party. When injected directly into the bloodstream, heroin causes a highly intense, very enjoyable rush of warmth to the abdomen. But playing with narcotics is like playing with fire. It's like speeding along in your car with your foot pressed down on the accelerator, surviving, and telling yourself, "Hey, I'll never crash." People who drive wildly often end up dead and people who use heroin often end up addicted.

Experienced users like to combine heroin with other drugs. Mixed with tobacco or marijuana heroin can be smoked. Some people enjoy injecting themselves with a mixture of heroin and cocaine. And yes, enjoy is the right word. Though some people quake at the mere sight of a hypodermic needle in a doctor's office many intravenous drug users seem to derive pleasure from the ritual of the injection itself. Addicts often share needles, an extremely dangerous practice and one of the major causes of the spread of the deadly AIDS virus.

Heroin can also be heated on tin foil and the vapors inhaled. Whether heroin is smoked, snorted, inhaled, injected under the skin, or into a muscle or vein, it almost invariably makes people sick at first. But just as many people who get sick the first few times they try alcohol go on to drink again, a lot of people who get sick when they try heroin try it again.

Eventually users stop feeling sick and experience pleasant sensations. But when tolerance develops this changes. People who inject themselves with heroin because they enjoy the warm rush the drug gives them soon find that the pleasant effects of heroin vanish with addiction. Addicts must get a dose of heroin every three to eight hours just to escape the unpleasantness of withdrawal.

In our society a heroin addict's life is dismal. Unless he's very rich he will have to find some way of making at least a hundred dollars a day to buy heroin. It's rough to come up with that kind of money even if you're a highly paid professional. When you're a teenager working at a supermarket, or a fast food restaurant, or pumping gas at the local gas station, forget it. Most of the ways teenagers can make big money fast aren't legal, and that includes selling drugs. Addicts are always in danger of being arrested not only for using illegal drugs but for what they have to do to get them.

The drug world is a violent place filled with danger. In the movies or on TV this can seem glamorous. In real life dealing with criminals is anything but fun. In addition to everything else addicts run the risk of dying either from an overdose or from contaminated drugs. The narcotics addict of a hundred years ago who went to a doctor and received a prescription for a specified dose of drugs safely produced by a pharmaceutical company has been replaced by the addict who must take his chances with unreliable street drugs. When heroin is bought on the street the dose varies wildly from too little to be effective to amounts which are potentially deadly. The addict has no way of knowing what he is injecting into his veins until it is too late.

By now you're probably wondering why every heroin addict doesn't run immediately to the nearest drug treatment center in search of a cure. Many do, but remember what we said earlier about addiction. It's extremely difficult to cure. Melodramatic as it may sound, addiction equals enslavement.

Methadone

One of the most effective ways of treating heroin addiction is with methadone. Methadone is a synthetic opiate. So methadone, too, is an addictive drug. Methadone has some advantages over heroin. It's taken orally, which eliminates the danger of contaminated needles. It doesn't provide much pleasure. That makes it a less seductive drug. Some addicts find that when they take methadone they don't crave heroin. It's given in controlled doses, so the chance of overdosing is minimal.

Would addicts fare as well or better on heroin maintenance programs? Or is methadone a way station which allows at least some addicts to overcome their heroin addiction and ultimately give up the milder methadone, too? What's more, even if addicts could be maintained on heroin aren't they better off on methadone? If there was good solid statistical information available on the results of drug treatment programs perhaps we could answer these questions. But the data just doesn't exist.

The number of people who drop out of all drug treatment

programs is very high. Many people who appear to be cured of a drug addiction go back to drugs. This may not happen for months or even years, which makes it hard to determine whether somebody who seems cured really is. At least we do know that methadone has permitted a number of addicts to lead normal lives while they're on methadone. All other methods of treatment of hard-core addicts have produced results which are dubious at best.

There are many theories about drug treatment and many kinds of treatment facilities. Good drug treatment centers generally provide users with a drug-free environment where there is structure and routine. Users receive some form of therapy—individual, group, and/or peer. Family therapy is also an important part of the program. Recreational and occupational activities help the user develop confidence and learn valuable skills. Ideally, users make friends in treatment centers and encounter warmth and understanding. Aftercare is usually an important component in the treatment plan. Some treatment centers favor a tough, even brutal approach to drug users. A few have evolved into near cult status, with addicts remaining permanently in the facility/community where presumably they remain drug-free. Whether they would stay off drugs if they left the center and had to cope with the world outside is open to question.

Of course, one of the biggest problems for drug users is returning to the same environment that led them to take drugs in the first place. All their anxieties can resurface again after treatment. If they're unhappy or can't find a job or if most of the people around them take drugs they may be tempted to try drugs once more.

Still, we want to stress that just as there are alcoholics who stop drinking and pull their lives together, so there are heroin addicts who give up drugs and stay off drugs.

In the abstract the heroin user most likely to benefit from a good nonmethadone program is a nonaddict, but in reality you can't tell in advance who can be cured of a drug habit and who can't. Any heroin addict who wants treatment should be encouraged to get it. Even if treatment fails it should be tried again. Who knows? Next time round things could work out.

Fortunately not everyone who takes drugs is a heroin addict. People who use less addictive drugs or who have only played around with narcotics occasionally have a good chance of benefiting from treatment. For some teenagers drugs aren't the central problem of their lives anyway, but only one component in an elaborate scheme of problems. Treatment holds a lot of hope for teens like this. If this sounds like you the best way to begin to get help is to talk to an adult you trust. Or call a drug hotline. Don't wait. The time to start making your life better is right now.

4

Cocaine— Energy and Glamor

Suppose all drugs were legal and advertised on TV. Okay, that's not going to happen. The main drug we're likely to see advertised on television in the future is the same one we see advertised now: beer. Television is loaded with commercials showing groups of ordinary people and retired athletes holding up frothy mugs of golden beer at sunset. But if other drugs were advertised, guess which would get the ultra-classy, ultra-glamorous promotion. You guessed it. Cocaine.

A beautiful model swathed in diamonds would appear on your TV screen. She'd tell you that cocaine is the drug of choice of the rich and famous. To prove it she'd drop the names of a rich movie star or two and one or two well-known major league baseball players who use cocaine. She'd show you cocaine. It's white and comes in crystalline or powder form, which explains why it's nicknamed "snow." On your TV screen it would look dazzling and glittery. Then the model would smile mysteriously and the commercial would fade away.

Even decades ago when Cole Porter penned the line "I

get no kick from cocaine," later changed to "I get no kick from champagne," for a song in his hit Broadway musical *Anything Goes,* cocaine was identified with glamorous sophisticated people off on a spree. As the comedian Richard Pryor (who used to have a serious drug problem) said a few year ago, "Cocaine is nature's way of telling you you're making too much money."

But cocaine is no longer the preferred drug of rich people alone. Cocaine has come down in price and is used by middle-class people. Recently, cocaine has caught on with the very poor in the form of crack. Crack is cocaine reduced to a small blackish lump and smoked in a pipe. It's cheap and provides a quick high.

Back in the nineteenth century cocaine was just another drug, another medication, when it captured the attention of John Styth Pemberton of Atlanta, Georgia, who marketed patent medicines. Pemberton had already successfully sold "Triplex Liver Pills" and "Globe Flower Cough Syrup" when he came up with "French Wine Coca—Ideal Nerve and Tonic Stimulant." Note the key words: coca and stimulant.

Coca is a shrub which grows on the eastern slopes of the Andes Mountains in South America. The shrub contains over a dozen drugs and cocaine is the most potent. Just so you don't get confused, coca has nothing whatsoever to do with cocoa or chocolate, which are made from the seeds (beans) of the cacao tree, not the coca shrub.

Cocaine is a stimulant. That means it stimulates and energizes the central nervous system. "French Wine Coca" was modeled on a European nerve tonic called Mariani's wine, a red wine to which coca was added. The coca in the wine did more than wake people up. It suppressed the appetite. When Pope Leo XIII became an ascetic late in life he drank Mariani's wine so he could endure extended periods of fasting without feeling desperately hungry.

In 1886 Pemberton decided to market a syrup which apparently contained both coca and an extract of kola nut. The kola nut contains caffeine. Pemberton combined the words coca and kola and named his new syrup Coca-Cola. The syrup was designed to alleviate a variety of ailments, including depression. Just how much coca the original Coca-Cola contained has always been a matter of dispute and rumor.

In the early part of the twentieth century the Coca-Cola Company switched to a decocainized (drug-free) extract of coca leaves which added only flavor. The caffeine remained.

The Origins of Cocaine

Most of the world first learned of cocaine in the sixteenth century, when Spanish invaders came upon a magnificent empire in what is now Peru. This was the empire of the Incas, rich in silver, gold, and coca leaves. Coca leaves were prized by the Indians, who chewed them to create a sense of euphoria.

When the Spanish conquered the Incas the Indians were set to work in the mines under brutal conditions. The Spanish allowed the Indians all the coca they wanted because coca made them better workers. Since the Indians received little food, coca gave them energy and helped kill hunger pangs. Because it's a stimulant coca may have eased depression, helping the Indians endure their suffering.

Drugs played a role in the conquest and subjection of the Indians of North America, too. In North America it was alcohol that profoundly affected the Indians. The Indians of South America at least had the advantage of being familiar with coca leaves. But to the Indians of North America alcohol was new and alien, a powerful drug introduced by European settlers. Some historians believe that alcohol so undermined tribal life that it made it easier to defeat the Indians. Once defeated the Indians found in alcohol a temporary escape. They drank to forget and to survive even though the effects of alcohol continued to be disastrous.

In Peru, Bolivia, and parts of Colombia coca leaves are still used. But the region of the high Andes is so poor coca leaves are more than a stimulant and a medicine. Coca is food. The leaves contain vitamins and minerals as well as drugs.

It takes a long time to chew coca leaves and the amounts of cocaine that enter the system this way are relatively low. So chewing coca leaves is much safer than taking cocaine in more concentrated forms. Because the Indians of the Andes have chewed coca leaves for centuries and ingest cocaine in its most natural form they are often held up as an example of a primitive people who have developed an ideal relationship with drugs. When they can't get enough food in their harsh environment they chew coca leaves and then they don't feel hunger. Coca helps them overcome fatigue. When they're sick or in pain coca leaves act as painkillers. People who favor legalizing drugs often point to the Indians of Peru and their wonderful coca shrub.

Frankly, we don't buy this. Coca may indeed be a source of comfort to the impoverished Indians of South America, but we can't help wondering if they wouldn't be better off with more food, easier lives, and medical treatment instead of coca leaves. As to the Indians' highly praised natural relationship to drugs, well, it's very easy to romanticize people who live in a faraway place and who have a very different culture. Up close things tend to look different. Besides, what does it say about a society when people must rely on drugs and alcohol to make life bearable?

In the late eighteenth and early nineteenth century the London slums were filled with people who drank enormous quantities of gin because gin was the only means of escape from a harsh reality. Yet most thoughtful people did not consider gin a blessing. It was viewed as a squalid by-product of poverty that allowed people to forget their troubles briefly but ultimately made things worse. Chewing coca leaves may be mild and benign compared to consuming huge quantities of gin, but even so the relationship between drugs and poverty raises serious ethical questions.

Although the high price of illegal drugs is a major cause of crime and most victims of crime are poor, many leaders in poor communities strongly oppose legalizing drugs. They're afraid that if drugs become legal, cheap, and widely available they'll be used to keep people passive and docile. They believe poor people need housing, jobs, and a better way of life, not self-destructive escapism in the form of drugs legally dispensed through clinics.

Though tonics containing coca were popular in America in the nineteenth century, for some reason chewing coca leaves never caught on. It can't just be esthetics, though cramming a wad of coca leaves in one's mouth, chomping away, and spitting out the residue isn't elegant. American men of the nineteenth century chewed tobacco, and if you've ever watched the manager of a baseball team on television spitting tobacco when the camera's on him you'll have to admit chewing tobacco isn't elegant either. Drugs are strangely quirky. Sometimes they catch on in one form, sometimes in another.

Though cocaine was first isolated from coca in the 1840s, decades passed before cocaine made its great contribution to medicine, specifically surgery. Experiments proved that when cocaine was injected near a patient's nerve the drug acted as a local anesthetic. Local anesthesia was inconceivable before the 1850s, when the hypodermic syringe was invented, and cocaine would become the very first local anesthetic in history. Cocaine proved especially effective in eye operations. Before the era of cocaine injections eye operations were almost unbearably painful.

One of the doctors who discovered that cocaine could be used as a local anesthetic became a cocaine addict by accident after injecting himself with the drug repeatedly during his experiments. We've already told the story of Dr. Halsted in the chapter on narcotics, since the doctor "cured" his cocaine habit by becoming a lifelong morphine addict. What happened to him wasn't all that rare in that breakthrough era of drugs and medicine. Anything new and experimental has its dangers, and doctors and nurses often found themselves unwittingly addicted to drugs because no one yet knew what drugs could do. Ironically, the wife of the man who invented the hypodermic needle became a morphine addict.

The most popular methods of using cocaine today are sniffing it or smoking it, so we don't usually associate the drug with hypodermic needles. To us needles mean heroin. But cocaine has always had a following among intravenous drug users. When Sir Arthur Conan Doyle chose to make his famous fictional detective Sherlock Holmes a cocaine user who injected the drug, Victorian readers didn't approve of Holmes's habit but they weren't shocked by it either. There were plenty of such users around.

Modern intravenous drug users often combine cocaine and heroin in a mixture called a speedball. Since heroin's a depressant and cocaine's a stimulant the drugs tend to enhance and soften each other's effects. A speedball gives you a strong high, but it curbs the agitation and tension that often come with cocaine alone.

Why do stimulants make people feel awake and alive? As you'd expect, there's more than one theory. Some experts believe that a dose of cocaine affects you the way a group of hungry wolves lunging for your throat would affect you. It puts your central nervous system on full alert and gets your body ready for a fight or flight.

Cocaine doesn't contain any magic energy. It mobilizes your own energy-releasing system. Instantly your body shuts down functions that in a crisis situation don't seem very important. For example, energy is shifted from your stomach and intestines to your brain, heart, and blood vessels. This may explain why some people lose their appetite when they take stimulants. Their bodies say, "Hey, this is no time to stuff your mouth, idiot. Here come the wolves. Run!"

When people are high on cocaine their heart beats faster and their blood pressure may rise. They may get the kind of nervous stomachache caused by extreme stress, which usually only hits people when they have to make a speech, play piano at a recital, face a key exam, or try out for a team. Along with an upset stomach they may get diarrhea.

Because the body can't operate at crisis pitch indefinitely people usually feel totally exhausted when the effects of cocaine wear off. One danger of cocaine is that users may try to overcome the fatigue and/or depression that follows a cocaine binge by taking more cocaine. Though they'll get high, they're really only exhausting themselves further while creating an increasing dependence on the drug.

Addicted or Dependent?

Cocaine is not an addictive drug in the sense that heroin and alcohol are addictive drugs. Heroin addicts and alcoholics must get regular doses of their drug or experience withdrawal symptoms which can be awful. Not so the cocaine user. Even someone accustomed to large amounts of cocaine will not get the shakes, throw up, sweat, or feel sick if he or she gives up the drug. But the classic pattern of addiction (craving, dependency, withdrawal) isn't the only possible form of addiction. People can become psychologically dependent on cocaine and feel a physical need for the drug. When they can't get it or voluntarily stop using it they often become deeply depressed.

In a sense someone hooked on cocaine is like someone hooked on cigarettes. Most cigarette smokers give up cigarettes without getting sick. But that doesn't mean the smoker will stay off cigarettes. Some ex-smokers become so frustrated, so unhappy, and so totally overwhelmed by their desire for tobacco that they start smoking again. Similarly, many people who try to give up cocaine miss the drug so much they return to it and keep returning to it no matter how many times they try to kick the habit. Call it drug dependency if you want, but it sure sounds like addiction to us.

People who use cocaine frequently develop a tolerance to the drug, which means they need increasingly higher doses to feel the sudden rush of euphoria that attracted them to the drug in the first place. So cocaine use tends to spiral upward in cost, time, and potential for abuse.

Of course, not everyone becomes euphoric on cocaine. Some people who use the drug just become jittery and irritable and/or have terrible bouts of insomnia. Anyone who smokes cocaine risks possible damage to the lungs and frequent sniffing of cocaine can irritate your nose.

Now some people do use cocaine for years (chiefly as a party drug) without problems. But it's seductively easy to slip into a massive cocaine habit. We'll sum up the reasons why. First, there are no withdrawal symptoms to signal abuse. Second, the more you take the more you need to get high. Third, the temptation to ward off the low that follows a high by getting high again is strong.

There's a fourth reason why cocaine is a seductive drug,

easy to abuse, and that is that the drug does what it's supposed to. It energizes! It stimulates! That's why cocaine appeals to some athletes and performers. Remember, cocaine is a drug which affects the nerves and muscles.

But does cocaine really help make an athlete stronger and more powerful? Can the drug increase endurance and heighten stamina? Even to ask these questions is to send a shiver of fear through many opponents of drugs who refuse to admit so much as the possibility that cocaine might improve an athlete's performance.

But wait a minute. Are we to believe that the cocaine which energizes and strengthens the Indians of South America somehow loses its power when North American athletes use it? There are many good reasons for not using cocaine. But we can't lie to ourselves and pretend that stimulants don't work. As we've said before, no drug is inherently good or bad and there is no such thing as a devil drug. Some athletes would probably be unable to function at all if they took cocaine before a game. Some actors (acting is a profession which takes hours of intense concentration and rehearsal) would never dream of having so much as a cup of coffee before standing in front of a camera or stepping onto a stage, much less cocaine. Like cocaine, coffee is a stimulant. Amphetamines are stimulants, too. Give amphetamines to some truck drivers on long-distance routes and they'd probably become too jumpy to climb behind the wheel. Hand amphetamines to some students cramming for an exam and they'd probably write sheer gibberish on their test papers the following morning.

But we have to recognize that stimulants (including the notorious cocaine) work for some athletes, some dancers, some actors, and some ordinary people trying to stay alert when what they really need is sleep. In a sense people turn to stimulants to do what really shouldn't be done, push one's body to the utmost. Nobody should drive all night. Nobody should rehearse to exhaustion. Nobody should leave studying to the last minute and have to cram. Athletes should derive all their energy from being in top condition.

Okay, that all sounds good, but nobody's perfect and nobody has total control over their lives. Sooner or later most people find themselves in a crisis which calls for extra energy. Even diligent, well-rested people who lead highly disciplined, orderly lives may find themselves needing a stimulant because the hours of their inner biological clock are out of sync with the schedule they have to follow. Some people's natural wide-awake hours run from midnight to five in the morning. What if they have a job which requires them to be at their liveliest and best from noon to five? They can't reset their biological clock, but a dose of stimulants can energize the body and get it moving.

We believe people should limit their use of stimulants to a moderate dose of caffeine in the form of coffee, tea, or soda. If they need something stronger they should consult a doctor. But we see why athletes might fall into the dangerous trap of relying on cocaine for energy. In our society we make heroes of athletes who win, so it's hardly surprising that some athletes will do anything to win.

Besides, athletes in our society are quite used to drugs. They're routinely subjected to all kinds of legal drugs from tranquilizers to sedatives to muscle relaxants to anesthetic sprays, ointments, anti-inflammatory drugs, and codeine, which is a narcotic. If you get a chance see the movie *North Dallas Forty.* It offers a revealing glimpse into the world of professional football, where athletes often play hurt, using large amounts of medication to dull the pain. To play hurt is to risk incurring a permanent injury, but athletes are expected to sacrifice themselves for the team, for stardom, for the fans, for the team owners, or because they're paid a lot of money.

If we immerse athletes in legal drugs which enhance performance we shouldn't be surprised when some cross the line and start using illegal drugs to excel. There are recorded cases of athletes using speedballs, amphetamines, and even heroin during competitions. And what about athletes who use steroids? We think steroids (which are popular with teenage boys, not just professional athletes) are so important we've devoted a whole chapter to them.

Isn't it hypocritical to focus primarily on cocaine and athletics, which is what the media sometimes do, when the real problem is deeper and more pervasive?

Can Cocaine Kill?

One last question remains. Can cocaine kill? It's a tough question to answer because cocaine is a street drug and nobody checks out what goes into street drugs. They're always potentially dangerous. But although as a rule stimulants rarely prove fatal, some deaths have been attributed directly to cocaine use.

Take the famous case of Len Bias. A student at the University of Maryland, Bias was the number one pro basketball draft pick of 1986, soon to play with his favorite team, the Boston Celtics. At age twenty-two, surrounded by some of his college teammates, Bias, who had been a regular cocaine user in seemingly perfect health, snorted cocaine at a party and died.

How could such a thing happen? We don't have all the facts about Len Bias and experts still debate the exact cause of his death, but there's no doubt that cocaine was the culprit. Recently, doctors and scientists have determined that some people are sensitive to cocaine or can become sensitive to cocaine. In sensitive users cocaine interferes with the electrical system of the brain and heart. This causes uncontrolled spasms of the heart muscle and/or constriction of the arteries. The result is cardiac arrest. To put it bluntly, you may be a healthy young person with a normal heart, but if you're cocaine-sensitive and don't know it, the first time you sniff cocaine you may die. Or you may use cocaine regularly, never have a moment's trouble with the drug, become cocaine-sensitive suddenly, sniff the drug, and wham! We don't mean to be alarmist. Sensitivity to cocaine is rare. But it is something to think about.

Doctor Freud's Habit

Putting cocaine to work as an energizing drug was first tried in Europe in 1883, when a German doctor distributed pure cocaine to soldiers on maneuvers to help them ward off fatigue. A young Austrian doctor learned of this experiment and since he was prone to depression and fatigue himself he decided to give cocaine a try. So he injected a moderate dose of the drug under his skin and was rewarded with a blast of euphoria. The doctor's name was Sigmund Freud; yes, the same Doctor Freud who later transformed psychiatry through his theory of psychoanalysis.

So delighted was Freud with the way cocaine seemed to turn bad moods into good moods that he gave the drug to his friend Dr. Ernst von Fleischl-Marxow (let's just call him Fleischl) who suffered from a disease of the nervous system. Chronic pain had driven Fleischl into a morphine addiction, and Freud hoped cocaine would curb Fleischl's craving for narcotics.

At first Freud's gift of cocaine seemed to do Fleischl good, and Freud wrote a jubilant letter to his wife-to-be describing the wonders of cocaine, which he now used regularly, and urging her to try the drug.

Freud found cocaine exhilarating. The drug gave him vitality, increased his muscular strength, helped him to work hard, built his confidence, and made him alert and quick-thinking, or so he believed. What's more Freud liked cocaine because unlike alcohol there was no "morning after" to contend with, no sickness, no hangover. Freud claimed he was in full control of the drug, that he never felt the slightest craving for it, and that he only took it when he was really in need of a lift.

When Freud published an essay extolling cocaine he soon found himself under attack. Medical researchers pointed out that everything Freud said about cocaine was true up to a point. But there were troubling aspects to cocaine. It wasn't the innocent wonder drug Freud thought it was. Some people seemed to go crazy on cocaine, hallucinating and becoming paranoid. Although Freud could resist cocaine some people became dependent on the drug. It seemed potentially addictive.

Freud received further proof of what cocaine could do by observing Fleischl's reactions to the drug. Because he was in constant pain Fleischl was soon taking large amounts of cocaine just as he'd once taken large amounts of morphine. After only a year on the drug he was up to a full gram a day, which was twenty times what Freud took occasionally. Fleischl was so badly hooked his habit cost him a fortune, and he had terrifying hallucinations, the kind alcoholics get when they suffer from delirium tremens. Fleischl saw and felt snakes crawling over his skin!

Speed freaks (people who inject large doses of amphetamines intravenously) also see imaginary snakes and insects. Sometimes speed freaks feel insects crawling over their skin. Worse yet, sometimes speed freaks feel insects crawling *under* their skin. Speed freaks often have open sores and scabs on their face and arms because they gouge at their skin to get at the unpleasant creatures they hallucinate.

Fleischl's condition persuaded Freud that cocaine was dangerous, and he soon stopped using the drug. He may have missed the benefits of cocaine but he never missed the drug itself and was never tempted to return it. But Freud watched Fleischl endure six more pain-racked and drug-plagued years before death freed him from his misery.

Would Freud have developed a drug problem if he'd continued to use cocaine? Who knows? Drugs affect different people differently, and there may be biochemical and genetic factors that protect some people from the negative aspects of drugs and make other people vulnerable. Freud may have mastered cocaine, at least in the short run, but he was hopelessly addicted to nicotine.

Freud smoked over twenty cigars a day for decades. When he was in his thirties a physician warned Freud to stop smoking because it wasn't good for his heart. Freud stopped but became very depressed. He was besieged by fantasies of people dying or deserting him with sad farewells. He couldn't stand it and within seven weeks he was smoking again.

Freud tried repeatedly to stop smoking in the years that followed and once succeeded for fourteen months. But he simply couldn't give up smoking. His heart grew worse. He developed cancers on his palate and jaw. By the time he was in his late seventies his jaw had been removed entirely and an artificial jaw substituted instead. All in all he underwent thirty-three operations for cancer. He was in constant pain. Sometimes he couldn't speak or even chew. But through all this he kept on smoking cigar after cigar all day. He died of cancer at age eighty-three. You never know when you start using a drug where it will take you.

Mitch

Now let's find out what it's like sniffing cocaine for someone your own age.

It was Thanksgiving and seventeen-year-old Mitch couldn't stand it. On television people always smile on Thanksgiving. It's supposed to be a holiday about family caring and having roots. But to Mitch it was always the longest, most boring, most dismal day in the year.

Every Thanksgiving his brother would fly in from Ohio with his wife and children, and his sister who was divorced would fly in from Maine with her children, and Mitch would get in the car with them and his mother and father and drive to his grandmother's where the house always swarmed with obnoxious children. The turkey was always overcooked and the pumpkin pie tasted awful. Mitch hated pumpkin pie.

His relatives would drone on and on about things Mitch had no interest in. If he tried to escape and watch football on television his mother would threaten him. If he brought his Walkman and listened to music his father complained. There seemed to be at least seventy hours in the day and he usually wound up having a fight with his parents when he got home because everybody's nerves were worn to shreds trying to spend a whole day being nice to each other.

This year was worse than usual. Mitch was tired because he'd worked overtime at the supermarket the day before and he hadn't gotten any sleep because his girlfriend broke up with him after work. She'd screamed at him. He almost hit her. Then she did hit him. Finally she threw his class ring at him and he stormed out of her house while she cried on the phone to her best friend.

Mitch glanced at his watch. In precisely one hour he'd be squashed in the car between two whining little kids and heading off to his grandmother's. Then the doorbell rang and standing in the doorway was Mitch's older cousin Stan, in town from Denver. Wasting no time, Stan (who apparently dreaded the day ahead as much as Mitch) offered Mitch some cocaine. Mitch had never tried cocaine. Every weekend he drank beer with his friends and maybe two or three times a year he'd smoke pot. He felt a little scared at the idea of taking cocaine but he was also flattered by Stan's offer.

Mitch brought Stan up to his room and locked the door so his parents couldn't come barging in. Stan took some white powder out of a bag. There was no mirror in the room so Stan grabbed a framed picture and slapped it down on the desk. Then he sprinkled the powder over the glass covering the picture, cut lines in the powder with a razor, rolled a twenty-dollar bill tightly, and sniffed up the powder, one line per nostril.

Now it was Mitch's turn. He had watched his cousin with great interest but for just a moment he hesitated, afraid the cocaine would irritate his nose or affect him in some bizarre way. He certainly didn't want to run amok in front of all his relatives.

But with Stan staring at him assuming he must have sniffed cocaine before Mitch couldn't very well back off, so he choked down excuses and sniffed. The cocaine didn't irritate his nose at all and suddenly, smash, wham, wow, his fatigue was gone. His mind was clear. He felt great.

Mitch insisted on driving his family to his grandmother's. The drive was a pleasure. He had never felt so alert, so in control. He also felt wonderfully secretive. The knowledge that he was high on cocaine made him feel smugly superior to the people around him.

Mitch had little appetite for Thanksgiving dinner and as the day went on he grew fidgety. Otherwise things were fine. It was turning into the most interesting Thanksgiving Day in memory.

That night Mitch was so wide awake and restless he couldn't get to sleep till 3:00 A.M. The next day when his mother woke him up to go to work he was exhausted and couldn't get out of bed. He had to call in sick, which really bothered him because he needed the money and if he didn't go to work he didn't get paid. He lay in bed, groggy and bored, and began thinking about yesterday. He had really liked cocaine. Today promised to be awfully tedious. All the worries he'd forgotten about when he took cocaine were back nagging at him. Should he call Stan and ask for more cocaine? He decided not to. Because he had enjoyed cocaine so much more than beer or pot he was a little afraid of it.

Besides, in only three more days he'd be back in school. He'd see his girlfriend there. They'd had fights before and made up. Maybe they'd make up again. Maybe he wouldn't wait till he got back to school. Maybe he'd call her today. Someday he'd consider trying cocaine again but not now and not soon. Though Mitch wouldn't dare admit it to anybody but himself he was glad his cousin Stan was leaving for Denver tonight and taking his cocaine with him.

5

Marijuana— Still Cheap, Still Available

It was Saturday night, party time at State College. It was Saturday night, party time at fifteen-year-old Lisa's suburban high school. At State College most of the party-goers were divided into two groups. One group was guzzling beer in the bars a short drive from campus. The other group, which included Lisa's older sister Holly, was in the dorms smoking pot.

A towel was shoved against the bottom of Holly's door. In the next room along the corridor a sheet hung from floor to ceiling, filling the doorway. Both towel and sheet served the same purpose. They were there to keep the pungent aroma of marijuana smoke from drifting along the corridor into the nose of any administrator of the college who happened to be passing that way.

For Lisa's friends in high school, party time usually meant beer or marijuana, too. Like Holly, Lisa would never dream of using cocaine, and again like Holly the very idea of ever sticking a needle full of heroin into her arm was enough to make her sick. Hard drugs would never be part of Holly's or Lisa's life.

Holly doesn't smoke marijuana often. Neither does Lisa. But tonight Cheryl, Lisa's best friend, has invited a few people over to smoke pot. Lisa had to think fast. Cheryl's parents are in Florida. If Lisa's mother found this out Lisa wouldn't be allowed to go to Cheryl's. Only hint that there will be no adults present at Cheryl's and Lisa's mother would suspect something, not necessarily marijuana but something. It was time to evolve a strategy.

Before we go any further understand that Lisa is not the rebel of the sophomore class nor is her mother the wicked witch of the west. When caught sneaking regular cigarettes or even slipping out to a drinking party Lisa usually meets anger but not panic. Drinking's officially taboo for teenagers like Lisa but just about everyone she knows drinks, at least once in a while. Her mother drinks. But her mother doesn't smoke pot.

As for Lisa herself, well, she certainly isn't a drug burnout case. In the top quarter of her class academically, Lisa is an art major who ran for student council (staying sort of calm when she didn't win), is on yearbook, girls' track, and for three weeks in the fall went out with a popular boy who's on the soccer team. What more could a mother ask?

Several conversations and a half-dozen notes round Spanish class later, Lisa came up with the plan of spending the night at Dawn's but sneaking out first to Cheryl's. There was a chance Lisa's mother would call Dawn while Lisa was out, and that might spell trouble, but it was a chance Lisa would have to take. It would be far riskier to spend the night at Cheryl's. Dawn would certainly do her best to cover up for Lisa no matter what happened.

Score points for strategy! Lisa made it to Cheryl's eager for a good time. Lisa had to admit to herself that so far her previous encounters with marijuana had been disappointing. The first time she smoked pot absolutely nothing happened. Nothing! The whole evening turned out to be boring beyond belief. The other times she tried marijuana she'd grown so tired all she could do was lie around until it was time to go home.

To Lisa's delight tonight was different. Getting high was making her giddy. Everything seemed funny. There was a throw rug on the den floor and one of the boys, Ted, pulled it over his head and barked like a dog. Cheryl gave everybody a stuffed animal and the group pretended the stuffed animals were puppets. The jokes got wilder, the conversation juicier. Lisa was having a great time.

As the night wore on a hunger attack swept over the group and they raided the kitchen, devouring chocolate cake, cheese, potato chips, whatever they could munch their way through. While snacking, Ted told Lisa that he never knew in advance how many joints it would take to get high. Sometimes half a joint was enough, sometimes two joints, sometimes more. Lisa, whose mouth was getting very dry, opened her third can of soda and told Ted about the time she and Holly had driven to a local hangout where drugs were sold. Then Ted told Lisa about the time he went to New York City's Washington Square Park. He'd been told it was *the* place to buy drugs and as he'd strolled slowly around the park several people had offered him cocaine, marijuana, you name it. Only he had to make sure the cops didn't see him buy any.

Cheryl, who wore contact lenses, interrupted Ted and Lisa to complain that her eyes felt dry. Ted told her not to worry. If her eyes got red just use eyedrops and tell people she was coming down with a cold. Lisa started giggling again and couldn't stop even when the phone rang. It was

Dawn warning Lisa that her mother was looking for her. It was time to move fast.

Ted said he'd drive Lisa to Dawn's. Lisa wasn't sure she should drive with Ted because he was high but Ted said smoking pot isn't the same as drinking. You can drive when you use pot. Anyways, how else could she get to Dawn's? If this were a drinking party Lisa knew she could call her mother. Okay, so her mother would be annoyed with her but she'd still come and get her. Lisa and her mother had discussed the "do's and don'ts" of drinking in great detail. Though her mother certainly didn't condone her getting drunk the biggest "don't" when it came to drinking was driving drunk or letting someone drunk drive.

Marijuana was something else again. Lisa's mother lumped all drugs together, from pot to coke and heroin, and Lisa was terrified of what her mother would do if she learned that she was high from smoking pot. There'd be no looking the other way, no mere idle threats, no week or so of being grounded for Lisa. There'd be war.

What if her mother got so mad she phoned the parents of every teen who was at Cheryl's? That would be humiliating. What if her mother found out where Cheryl's parents were and phoned them in Florida? What if her mother forbade her going to the sophomore dance? "What ifs" by the dozen flashed through Lisa's mind. She decided to risk driving with Ted. But oh to be free like Holly and Holly's friends Jeff and Beth. Lisa had enjoyed a couple of marijuana-soaked weekends with them when she visited her sister at State.

At State College Holly was in a deeply relaxed mood, happily smoking pot and listening to music. Jeff and Beth were with her. Jeff's nickname around the dorms was "the dealer." Beth's room was the one next door with the massive sheet hanging across the doorway.

Enjoying It Less

Unlike Holly, Beth wasn't having fun. She had started using marijuana in her freshman year of high school and for a while she used marijuana strictly at parties. Now marijuana is not like tobacco. Most of Beth's friends in high school went from their first cigarette (inhaling) to a pack-and-a-half habit in weeks, sometimes only days. It takes a lot longer to become dependent on marijuana than regular cigarettes. So marijuana as a problem sort of sneaked up on Beth.

Beth was well aware that many people who use marijuana don't become dependent on it. Look at Holly. She smoked pot from time to time, always with friends, and she was okay. She would probably never move beyond a level she could handle. But marijuana affects different people differently, and though Beth hadn't meant to overdo it she just slipped into smoking pot heavily. The more she smoked the less pleasure she got out of pot and the greater the quantity she needed to feel good. She got used to doing ordinary things smoking pot. At one time Beth would never have dreamed of using marijuana just before going to class, or going to the launderette, or cooking, or driving, or riding a bicycle. Now pot was just part of the normal routine of her life.

She smoked joints alone now as well as when other people were around. She was smoking earlier too, starting in the morning. She knew she should cut back. Marijuana was supposed to be easier to cut back on than tobacco. Maybe that was true physically but psychologically Beth was finding it very hard.

She worried about the long-term effects of heavy marijuana use. The tars in cigarette smoke were a known health hazard. Surely the tars in marijuana smoke couldn't be good for your lungs. And then there was this rotten cough. She couldn't get rid of it any more than many cigarette smokers can get rid of theirs. The high she once loved was gone. Half the time she walked around feeling like someone had given her a sedative. Face it. She was no longer in control of her marijuana "habit." The "habit" controlled her.

Holly smiled, dreamily stoned. Beth sighed, and lit another joint.

Let's say goodbye to Holly and go back to Lisa. Let's plunk Lisa down at the kitchen table across from her mother. It's about time they had a little talk. Things are in a bad way when Lisa would risk driving home with someone who's stoned rather than phone her mother and ask for a ride.

Lisa puts her argument this way: Look, marijuana is so popular it doesn't even seem like a drug. Smoking a joint's like drinking a glass of spiked punch at a party. Everyone does it. Well, not everyone, but everyone worth knowing. There are a few prissy bores who don't drink or smoke pot but nobody at school wants to be like them.

Lisa's mother counters with, hey, no ifs, ands, or buts, marijuana isn't spiked punch. It's a drug and it's doubly treacherous because it leads to heroin. Marijuana's smoked by nasty types who wear dirty jeans and listen to heavy metal rock. You'll wind up hanging around with the wrong crowd if you smoke pot. So don't give me this everybody does it. I don't want to hear it. I don't want to hear about your sister smoking pot either. She shouldn't. But she's older than you and she's out of the house. You're not in college. You're in high school. You didn't go out with boys when you were twelve. You were too young. You go out with them now because you're old enough. I don't think you're old enough to mess around with anything as dangerous as pot.

Sighing deeply, Lisa repeats that everybody, not just the "wrong crowd" smokes pot. As for leading to heroin most people who use heroin tried alcohol as well as pot. But nobody goes around saying alcohol leads to heroin use. As for being too young, parents always think kids are too young for everything. Why do parents always sound like something out of *Reefer Madness?* Don't they know how funny that movie is? Instead of scaring kids, *Reefer Madness* is on every teen's list of all-time funny films. Besides, here we are at the kitchen table drinking coffee. Some people start the day off with a headache until they get their morning jolt of coffee. Coffee makes people jumpy. Pot is relaxing. It's fun. Why is pot worse than coffee?

Lisa's mother has gone from glaring to raging. What about the people who can't handle marijuana? (Lisa remembers Beth.) There are plenty of people who think they can handle alcohol who wind up alcoholics. There are people who believe they've got drugs under control, too, who find out the hard way they don't. Ignore the talk about how you can do anything when you're stoned and you'll be just fine. That's silly. Some people brag about driving stoned, flying planes stoned! But people used to say the same things about alcohol. How many people once thought they could drive safely after a drink or two? How many people thought cigarettes were harmless thirty years ago? Turns out tobacco's anything but harmless. And shut up about coffee. You're not going to be arrested for going to the supermarket and buying a can of Maxwell House.

Lisa's mother's voice has risen to a shout. Lisa rushes off to her room and slams her door. But she gives her mother one parting shot. Drugs make you feel good. Adults don't like to admit it but it's true. The real reason we teens use drugs is because we like the way drugs make us feel. Grown-ups don't understand that.

Now Lisa's in her room upset and her mother's in the kitchen brooding. What they both need is to cool down and sift through the facts, the distortions, and the rumors about marijuana. To begin with, what is marijuana anyway?

A Remarkable Plant

Cannabis sativa, also called hemp, is a plant. It's a remarkable and versatile plant which provides among other products a strong fiber used to make linen, canvas, and rope. The seeds of the plant (sterilized) are sold as bird feed. Many a canary has thrived on the seeds of *Cannabis sativa.* This has led to innumerable jokes about birds getting high, but despite the canary jokes marijuana doesn't come from the seeds of the plant. Cannabis also provides a linseed-like oil which when added to paints makes them dry faster.

Marijuana is made by drying the leaves and flowering tops of the plant. The flowering tops exude a sticky resin. When the resin alone is dried you get hashish, which is more potent than marijuana. The most active chemical in the resin is THC, which stands for the unpronounceable tetrahydrocannabinol. THC has been produced in modern laboratories as a synthetic and both THC and marijuana have medicinal uses.

Despite synthetic THC, marijuana is no new-fangled designer drug. *Cannabis sativa,* which probably originated in Asia, has been cultivated since ancient times. The plant is extremely hardy and spreads quickly. Unless measures are deliberately taken to stamp it out it flourishes in abandoned fields and along roadsides. Because it's easy to grow and abundant, marijuana is usually an inexpensive and easily available drug. In some countries it's the drug of choice of people too poor to buy alcohol. This link to the poor in many cultures gave marijuana the reputation of being a lowly, unglamorous weed. By and large middle-class Americans shunned marijuana until the 1960s when pot (one of marijuana's many nicknames) caught on with college students and with soldiers fighting in Vietnam.

In America marijuana is usually smoked in pipes and in the form of cigarettes called joints. But the drug can also be eaten. Whether the drug is eaten or smoked depends in part on how potent it is. In India *bhang,* a mild preparation of marijuana, is often diluted with water and drunk in beverage form. Bhang is sometimes even added to ice cream. If that seems strange remember we serve coffee ice cream and desserts flavored with highly alcoholic liqueurs.

In contrast *ganja* is a very strong marijuana preparation which includes resin. You may have heard of the Rastafarians of Jamaica. They wear their hair in a style called dreadlocks and their reggae music is famous throughout the world. Smoking ganja has an almost mystical significance to Jamaica's Rastafarians. From bhang to ganja! Just as alcohol isn't simple and predictable, neither is marijuana.

If two people smoke marijuana one may find the drug so stimulating he can't get to sleep that night while the other may grow very tired. Of course, small doses of marijuana cause less trouble than large doses. If someone isn't used to marijuana a strong dose may make him feel panicky. A strong dose may also make one grouchy or depressed. In extreme cases marijuana can make people feel disoriented and delirious, as if they have a fever, and disorientation is often followed by stupor.

Some people deliberately use marijuana to become disoriented. They view marijuana as a kind of mild hallucinatory drug. But marijuana is not a hallucinogen and when people become disoriented from smoking marijuana it usually just means they've overdosed. And the result is by no means always mild. Marijuana overdoses aren't fatal, but even plain heavy pot smoking can make you feel next day as if your mind has grown a coat of fuzz overnight. It isn't uncommon for beginners or even regular users to become groggy or irritable even on small doses of marijuana.

Is It Safe?

Still, just as there are people who drink sensibly and know when to stop there are people who smoke marijuana for years, enjoy it, and don't have any problems with it. There are also many people who try marijuana, smoke it awhile, give it up, and that's that. One of the biggest problems with marijuana is that people often mix pot with alcohol or other drugs. When you mix drugs you never know how the combination will affect you. Street drugs, of course, are always scary. Joints are sometimes sold to the unwary laced with PCP. If you want to know what PCP does to users read the chapter on hallucinogenic drugs. With any illegal drug you don't know what's in it, what's been done to it, or where it's been.

Normally marijuana is not toxic, but zealous opponents of the drug sometimes turn marijuana into a health hazard by seeing to it that fields of marijuana are sprayed with poisonous chemicals. For example, in the mid-seventies the U.S. government sponsored a program in which the herbicide paraquat was sprayed over marijuana growing illegally in Mexico. Farmers harvested the plants anyway and the contaminated marijuana found its way into the United States, where it was sold on the streets.

The spraying caused quite a furor. Even many people who were strongly opposed to marijuana were alarmed. The spraying was stopped, but large numbers of worried users responded by growing their own marijuana. Contaminating marijuana seems a brutal and dangerous way of fighting drug abuse but there is no guarantee that it won't be tried again in the future.

When people categorize drugs as good or bad they become victims of a kind of tunnel vision. Marijuana does, after all, have medicinal benefits. THC and marijuana have been used to treat menstrual cramps, vomiting, and headaches. Cancer patients on chemotherapy have used marijuana to ease the nausea caused by the therapy. Some patients suffering from the eye disease glaucoma have been permitted to smoke marijuana cigarettes legally. Apparently, marijuana reduces the fluid pressure which builds up in the eyes of people with glaucoma. In the nineteenth century marijuana was used in the treatment of a vast range of diseases including asthma. Newer, more potent drugs have eclipsed marijuana, but it still has its medical uses.

To show you just how long marijuana's been around, consider that the Assyrians and Persians were familiar with it. References to it are found in early Chinese and Indian writings. Early on the drug made its way to Africa. Marijuana was well known to the ancient Greeks, who didn't use it, preferring alcohol, but who traded with peoples who ate marijuana and who inhaled the drug's vapors.

Though in our society marijuana is usually smoked rather than eaten, some people do add it to food. The danger with eating marijuana is that it's hard to estimate just how much you're getting. It's easy to overdose when you eat the drug. Marijuana also works more slowly when it's eaten and most users want to get stoned fast. So they smoke joints.

In nineteenth-century Europe marijuana eating enjoyed a brief vogue among bohemians and artists. In Paris a group of famous French poets and writers formed the Club de Hachichins and published florid descriptions of what it felt like to devour large amounts of strong marijuana. Cannabis had been grown in Europe since at least the late Middle

Ages for fiber. Naturally, some Europeans growing cannabis also used marijuana, but like the Greeks most Europeans preferred alcohol.

Cannabis reached South America in the sixteenth century. By the seventeenth century the plant was cultivated in both Virginia and New England. Hemp was a major crop at the time of the American Revolution. George Washington grew the plant at Mount Vernon, presumably for its fiber, though he may have been interested in its medicinal aspects as well. The idea of the father of our country growing pot has led to many an irreverent joke among the stoned.

Hemp production declined after the Civil War but it didn't vanish. Hashish houses soon sprang up in several major American cities and in a few places, New Orleans for example, marijuana became quite popular. Poor blacks in the South smoked marijuana, as did Mexican immigrants. In the twentieth century "reefers" became popular with jazz musicians.

From the twenties on there were occasional newspaper accounts about "crazed marijuana fiends," but the drug was so identified with the poor, with minorities, and with outcast musicians that it wasn't perceived as a mainstream threat. Alcohol was much more fiercely attacked as a danger to society than marijuana. This doesn't mean that marijuana was ignored. Antimarijuana campaigns did occur, and by the late 1930s marijuana was illegal in most of the United States. Marijuana's reputation followed it into the sixties when it was again identified with outcasts and rebels, this time hippies and political radicals.

By the end of the sixties all kinds of people smoked marijuana. No longer an outcast drug, it seemed to be the one illegal drug that had a chance of being legalized. We discuss the arguments for and against legalizing drugs elsewhere in this book. The bottom line is marijuana hasn't been legalized. It's still a street drug. Using it is a risky business.

Though marijuana in one form or another has been around for centuries, the long-term effects are not well known. Remember, it took decades before the long-term health effects of cigarettes were known, and cigarettes were legal and carefully monitored. It's harder to study marijuana use. Some studies seem to indicate that heavy long-term marijuana use may produce basic alterations in personality, changes in the physical structure of the brain, even produce genetic damage. All of these alarming possibilities are just that—possibilities—not well established medical facts. The studies may turn out to be exaggerated or simply wrong —that often happens. But it is fair and reasonable to assume that smoking anything—marijuana or tobacco—simply can't be good for your health, and the more you smoke the worse it will be.

Surveys indicate that the popularity of marijuana among teens has declined rather sharply in recent years. But it's still very much around. It's still cheap, still available and remains, next to alcohol, the drug of choice for young Americans.

6
Hallucinogens— The Drugs of the Sixties

Name the decade and era idealized on college campuses across the country. If you said the sixties give yourself an *A*. A lot of young people would like to be transported back to a summer day in Washington Square Park in Greenwich Village in, say, 1966, or to San Francisco's famous Haight-Ashbury in 1967. Whatever the sixties were really like the image of the era is sheer magic to many. The decade evokes a time when young people were free, bold, and adventurous.

Flower children in colorful clothes, words like groovy and psychedelic, the Woodstock Festival in upstate New York, parties where teenagers smoked pot and drank Kool-Aid, astrology, communes, the sexual revolution, antiwar demonstrations—it's easy to conjure up the sixties. The movie *Easy Rider* sums up the sixties charisma about as well as anything, and central to the film is the romance of drugs.

This book is not the place to argue the pros and cons of the sixties or to try to determine what it was really like back then and what is merely nostalgia now. But no book about drugs can ignore the sixties. In the fifties middle-class teenagers generally stayed with alcohol. By the sixties they were using marijuana and other drugs. Though the media exaggerated the number of kids dropping out in the sixties and turning on to drugs, the mystique was certainly there. Drugs had acquired an aura of romance and one drug in particular was bathed in a golden glow. It wasn't speed. It wasn't pot. It was LSD, lysergic acid diethylamide, otherwise known as acid.

Even the all-time catchy descriptive word for and of the sixties, "psychedelic," comes from hallucinogenic drugs, and that's what LSD is, the key hallucinogenic drug. Psychedelic means "mind-expanding." Hallucinogenic drugs were supposed to do exactly that, expand your mind, alter your consciousness. So romanticized was LSD in the sixties that countless teenagers believed the Beatles song "Lucy in the Sky with Diamonds" was really about an LSD experience (called a trip) with the capital L, S, and D of the title a kind of secret code. Though the Beatles denied this the rumor persisted. Some people who used LSD claimed the drug really did produce beautiful visual effects like seeing diamonds. They also claimed that the drug permanently altered the way they felt about life. LSD had given them a bond with the world, a oneness with the universe, a form of "cosmic consciousness" they had never experienced before.

Many nonusers claimed that LSD was a very dangerous drug that could lead to bad trips, panic, madness, and even suicide. Diamonds! Panic! No wonder LSD fascinated teenagers in the sixties. As described by both its defenders and detractors LSD was legendary, the stuff of dreams, positively supernatural.

Of course, if LSD delivered even half of what it promised or was promised for it by users, it would never have been eclipsed by other drugs. Yet LSD has been at the mercy of fads and fashions the same as any other drug and though it's still around it's not nearly as popular as it used to be.

On the other hand the myths about LSD run both ways. For example, the drug does not drive people to suicide. Yes, some deeply depressed people and people with a history of mental illness who have taken LSD have also committed suicide. But there is no proof that LSD caused the suicides. LSD has also been accused of causing permanent chromosomal damage. There is little evidence to support either this or the claim that LSD drives people crazy. LSD *can* cause spontaneous abortions in pregnant women. Of course pregnant women should be wary of all drugs including caffeine, alcohol, and tobacco.

As with any new drug, any new substance, LSD may produce harmful long-term effects that have not yet been discovered. The drug may also have an as-yet-undiscovered potential for doing good. For years it was legal for psychiatrists to study LSD. Psychiatrists theorized that LSD was a drug that mimicked psychotic symptoms. They tested the drug to see if this were true. They also tested the drug to see if it made patients more receptive to therapy. They took LSD themselves to gain rapport with their patients and to learn whether the drug provided insights into the way the mind works. Unfortunately, the government clamped down on legitimate LSD research when the drug hit the streets, and many potentially interesting research projects were halted.

While the drug was simply a research tool of highly disciplined, law-abiding, well-educated, middle-class doctors and other professionals, the media paid relatively little attention to it. Experiments were conducted quietly without much fuss. The LSD available to researchers was very pure. It was made at the Sandoz Laboratories in Switzerland where the drug had been developed in 1938. Although experiments were ultimately inconclusive, doctors learned some useful things about the way the drug works. They found out that it's very scary to be left alone when taking LSD. Taking the drug in pleasant surroundings with friendly people present is one way of warding off a bad trip. Primitive peoples had learned the same thing about hallucinogenic drugs centuries ago. Let's take a closer look at hallucinogenic drugs in general.

To begin with the word *hallucinogenic,* like the word *psychedelic,* is really inaccurate. The drugs don't produce true hallucinations. As for "expanding the mind," that's not a clear descriptive phrase. It can mean different things to different people. Still, until someone comes up with a better name for them we'll use the term hallucinogenics. A hallucination is something you see and believe to be real that doesn't exist. Alcoholics undergoing delirium tremens (the dreaded DTs) have true hallucinations. They see snakes, insects, and other things they'd much rather not see which are entirely real to them.

By and large people using LSD see real objects, only the objects are distorted. Go to an amusement park and look in a distorting mirror. You'll see your actual reflection but the image will be elongated or blocky or weird in some other way. You know that what you're looking at is an illusion. LSD users usually know that the distorted objects they see are illusions, too.

In a little while we're going to introduce you to a teenager who took LSD but first we want to describe to you one of the most accurately recorded LSD trips ever taken. Dr. Albert Hofman, the co-discoverer of LSD, was a chemist at the Sandoz Laboratories. In 1943 Dr. Hofman was in the midst of studying LSD when a curious thing happened. Bear in mind that in those days there were no pro- or anti-LSD groups to bias Dr. Hofman's judgment. He had no preconceived ideas about the drug, no false expectations. He was a careful researcher and kept detailed notes about what happened, notes which were written down promptly while his memory was fresh.

What happened to Dr. Hofman that day in 1943 was an accidental LSD trip. While at work Dr. Hofman began to feel dizzy and restless. He assumed he was getting sick and went home. Once home he fell into a dreamy semiconscious state which he found entirely pleasant. The daylight streaming through his window seemed so bright he closed his eyes and discovered that with his eyes shut, "fantastic visions of extraordinary realness and with an intense kaleidoscopic play of colors assaulted me. After about two hours this condition disappeared."

Dr. Hofman wondered if somehow he'd ingested (eaten) the chemicals he'd been working with that day and if the chemicals had caused this strange experience. To test his theory Dr. Hofman decided to deliberately ingest the drug. What Dr. Hofman could not possibly know was how potent the new drug was. Because LSD is a synthetic substance it's many times more powerful than natural hallucinogenic drugs. LSD can produce effects in doses as small as twenty-five micrograms. A microgram is one millionth of a gram, and there are twenty-eight grams in an ounce. To give you an example of just how tiny that is, an average postage stamp weighs in the vicinity of sixty thousand micrograms.

Dr. Hofman gave himself what he thought was a very small dose of LSD, one quarter of a milligram. Actually one quarter of a milligram is an enormous dose. Poor Dr. Hofman. He spent the next six hours of his life on a memorably awful trip.

After Dr. Hofman took the drug he opened his notebook and waited patiently to see what would happen. Forty minutes later he began laughing uncontrollably. He tried to take notes but couldn't. The events of the day would have to be recorded later. All he wanted to do now was get home.

Accompanied by his laboratory assistant, Dr. Hofman bicycled home while things grew stranger by the minute. He found he couldn't speak clearly, and though he was convinced he wasn't moving he was actually bicycling very fast. The faces of the people around him "appeared as grotesque, colored masks." His throat was dry. He thought he was choking. His body seemed filled with lead.

Oddly, despite this heavy feeling it seemed to him he was actually out of his body, a neutral observer watching himself babble and shout. A medical doctor was called in to examine Dr. Hofman once he got home. All the doctor found wrong with the chemist was a weak pulse.

After about six hours the effects of the drug tapered off, but objects were still distorted, "like the reflections in the surface of moving water." They kept changing colors, too, but the colors weren't bright and jewel-like. They were "sickly green and blue." When he closed his eyes Dr. Hofman saw fantastic images. He experienced sounds as if they were visual sensations, each tone or noise evoking a colored picture. The sound/pictures kept changing in form and color. It was like looking into a kaleidoscope.

The next day, though Dr. Hofman was excessively tired he felt fine. As far he could tell LSD produced no aftereffects. Later, other LSD experiments would confirm what Dr. Hofman described. LSD trips generally last from six to twelve hours. The size of the dose can affect the experience. Users usually close their eyes once the drug starts to take effect. This enhances the visual imagery brought on by LSD.

People using LSD usually lie down when they take the drug. It's the safest thing to do. Obviously, driving a car or even going for a walk can be highly dangerous. LSD is not addictive, though any drug used regularly may lead to some kind of psychological dependency. Ordinarily, LSD is not the sort of drug one takes every day or even every week or every month. Tolerance for LSD builds up so quickly that if it's taken too often the effects are diminished.

Some people claim LSD causes flashbacks—that users may re-experience portions of a trip weeks, months, or even years after the trip is over. Many experts believe flashbacks are merely vivid memories, recollections of something seen or heard while having an LSD experience.

Untold centuries ago the Indians of South America began using natural hallucinogenic drugs, incorporating them into religious ceremonies. When the Spanish conquered Mexico they tried to wipe out this "sinful" practice but were unable to. Once any drug, including alcohol, is ingrained in a culture, it's very hard to get rid of.

The Indians had discovered that the crown of the small spineless cactus peyote (in Aztec, *peyotl*) when dried forms a hard "button." This is called a mescal button. You hold a mescal button in your mouth until it's softened. Then you swallow it. It tastes bitter and can make you throw up. One may have to devour as many as six to twelve buttons before a hallucinogenic experience occurs. Usually the nausea subsides first.

In the nineteenth century peyote use spread to the Indians of North America. Again attempts were made to suppress peyote and again the attempts failed. Many legal battles have been fought over the Native American Church practice of using peyote in religious rituals.

In the late nineteenth century scientists isolated the main hallucinogenic ingredient in peyote—mescaline. Mescaline causes nausea but it doesn't last as long as the nausea caused by peyote. The writer Aldous Huxley tried mescaline and wrote a book about his experience with the drug in

1954. The book is called *Doors of Perception*. Long before Huxley experimented with mescaline numerous intellectuals, philosophers, and even clergymen had experimented with peyote, lured by the idea of achieving a mystical religious experience.

Cactus plants are not the only source of natural hallucinogens. Ages ago the Indians of Mexico discovered mushrooms containing psilocybin, a hallucinogenic substance. Dubbed "magic mushrooms" in the sixties, "shrooms" found a following in the drug culture. Though it is obviously dangerous to go around picking mushrooms if you don't know what you're doing (only experts can spot which are safe and which can kill you) some enthusiasts did go in search of hallucinogenic mushrooms in Mexico in the sixties and seventies. For a while kits containing spores of the mushrooms were sold by mail. Mushrooms could be grown from the spores.

Certain varieties of morning glory seeds can cause hallucinogenic experiences. However, morning glory seeds make people so violently ill it might be more fun trying to alter your consciousness by repeatedly banging yourself on the head with a baseball bat.

Ground nutmeg is a spice found in most kitchens which has the reputation of being mildly hallucinogenic. But it must be consumed in large quantities to have any effect at all and in such high amounts nutmeg makes people extremely sick. Kids should leave nutmeg where it belongs, in pumpkin pies.

One well-known drug commonly confused with hallucinogens is PCP, angel dust. PCP was developed in a laboratory in the late fifties and was originally sold as an anesthetic. PCP (phencyclidine) was given to patients during surgery. The drug did not make patients lose consciousness. Instead it made them feel disassociated. Patients had at least some awareness of what was being done to them in surgery but they felt distanced from it, uninvolved.

At first doctors welcomed the drug as a major medical breakthrough in anesthesia, but as so often happens with miracle drugs and wonder drugs PCP wound up a disappointment. The out-of-body sensation the drug caused was too much for most patients, who found it very disturbing. In 1965 the drug was withdrawn—for humans, that is. In 1967 the drug was made available to veterinarians as an anesthesia for animals.

Oddly enough, when word got around that PCP was good for animals undergoing surgery but not for people undergoing surgery PCP lost prestige as a street drug. For years PCP was viewed in the drug culture as a second-rate drug, a mere "animal tranquilizer." Dealers fobbed it off on gullible buyers who thought they were getting fancier stuff. PCP comes in pill form as well as powder form but it's as a powder that it finally caught on, under the pretty name "angel dust."

In the late seventies and early eighties television discovered angel dust. It's hard to determine how many people were using PCP at the time and how many of those who used it were teenagers. TV news shows claimed the drug was popular with kids and the drug either became more popular with kids thanks to all the publicity or just seemed more popular. Anyway, for a time PCP was in the news. Then, as is the way with television, the media turned its cameras away from PCP and onto another drug, in this case cocaine.

Mixing drugs is very common, and PCP users often sprinkle angel dust on marijuana to create a potent cigarette (joint). Sometimes users snort the drug. PCP makes people feel passive and disconnected from their surroundings. The drug can make people feel dizzy and nauseous. It affects muscular coordination and users often find that their legs feel rubbery. Like LSD, PCP can make users temporarily paranoid.

To Derrek, 17, PCP sounded like a boring drug. LSD seemed interesting. He had checked around and asked a lot of questions about different kinds of drugs. Because he loves music and had been told that listening to music when you've taken LSD is a mystical experience, he decided to try it. Several of his friends suggested he try cocaine, but to Derrek cocaine symbolizes everything that's wrong with the world. He had given the subject a lot of thought and decided that cocaine was a symbol of a frenzied age. It was the drug for people hustling after fast money and fast thrills. LSD, with its sixties connotations, seemed to promise a meaningful experience.

Derrek lives in Hyde Park, a neighborhood on the South Side of Chicago, where the University of Chicago is located. He lives in an apartment with his mother, who works as a waitress, and his two younger sisters. Contrary to the myths about teenagers who try drugs, Derrek is (a) not a poor student, (b) not a criminal, (c) not trying to solve his personal problems through drugs. Derrek is a B-plus student at his high school, works part-time in a supermarket to earn extra money, gets on with his mother, and keeps in close touch with his father (his parents are divorced) who lives in California. Like many teens, Derrek tried drugs because drugs are widely available, he knew other teenagers who'd tried drugs, and he was curious about them.

LSD can be synthesized in a fairly simple chemistry lab and the chemicals required aren't hard to get. Because LSD is effective in minuscule doses it's available in an amazing range of forms. LSD has been sold deposited on sugar cubes and on animal crackers. It comes in tablets, gelatine chips, on pieces of paper stamped with ink designs containing the drug, and on pieces of paper that have been soaked in the drug. (It was widely rumored that decals with a picture of Mickey Mouse on them contained the drug. The rumor apparently was untrue.)

Before trying LSD Derrek tried mescaline. He had been told by a friend that he should start with mescaline and "work his way up" to LSD. When Derrek felt ready for LSD he got it through a friend who knew somebody who knew somebody who knew somebody who could obtain LSD. Derrek and Gary, a close friend, tried LSD together. They enjoyed a calm, pleasant trip, listening to music.

The next time Derrek took LSD he and Gary swallowed it quickly on the run outside. Someone was on their trail. Not the cops. Not Derrek's mother. The reason for their haste was that they were trying desperately to escape from a couple of fourteen-year-old girls who wanted to take LSD, too. The boys (then sixteen) were convinced they'd wind up "babysitting" the girls, especially if LSD made the girls feel panicky.

This time Gary and Derrek were more psyched up about LSD than they were the first time around. As the drug started to take effect, the ground seemed to tilt inward, making them feel as if they were walking inside a cylinder. Moving objects left a blur behind them like a comet's tail. It was something Derrek and Gary had seen in rock videos, but that was a mere special effect. This was for real, or so it seemed. Again the boys lucked out. They made it home safely and sat around listening to music.

Derrek's third trip was considerably more dramatic, so dramatic he still remembers the exact date. He was at home with three friends. Derrek's mother was working and his sisters were visiting relatives so he and his friends had the apartment to themselves.

Derrek believes he was permanently transformed during this trip, that his "perception expanded to infinity." He describes hearing a voice saying, "Life is just one big constant pleasure experience, and all bad things are merely an illusion and don't exist." To Derrek the words provided a "mythic insight into true reality."

Derrek claims that on this trip he saw multiple bright colors passing through rings of light, that he felt himself flying through a psychedelic universe. Hellish fire surrounded him and he saw demons. Suddenly he leaped up, tore off his clothes and ran to his room, screaming, "Pleasure, pleasure, pleasure!"

At this point Derek's friends, who were just sitting around talking, became scared. Nervously, they debated what to do. When Derrek burst into hysterical laughter they rushed upstairs and locked him in his room. The laughter continued. By now they felt totally helpless and scared. Would Derrek hurl himself out a window? Would he crash into something and injure himself by accident? Would he make so much noise the neighbors would call the cops? One of Derrek's friends went to the phone and called for an ambulance. The ambulance came and Derrek was given a sedative and rushed to the hospital. There the trip ran its course.

When an exhausted Derrek awoke, the first thing he saw was his mother standing at the foot of the hospital bed. She was no illusion. She yelled at him, uttering dire threats. To make matters worse she'd phoned his father, who was flying in from California. Derrek knew he was in for some very rough times.

What happened to Derrek? Why did he have such an extreme reaction to LSD? It may have been the dosage. Remember what happened to Dr. Hofman when he inadvertently took too strong a dose of LSD. Derrek got his drugs from a friend who knew somebody who knew somebody who knew somebody who sold LSD. Street drugs are often adulterated and contaminated. LSD is sometimes mixed with amphetamines, even strychnine. Derrek had little to go on besides blind faith that the LSD he bought was safe. Since different drugs affect different people differently it's possible for one person (Derrek) to have a bad reaction to a drug while other people (Derrek's friends) react mildly to it.

Did Derrek really see demons and bright colors passing through rings of light, or is he exaggerating things? Remember why Dr. Hofman's account of his LSD experience is so valuable. Dr. Hofman was a trained researcher. He had no preconceived notions about LSD and what it might do. He wrote about his LSD experience in great detail as soon as the experience ended.

A whole year passed between the time Derrek took LSD and the time we interviewed him about it. We weren't the first people to hear about Derrek's trip. He told a lot of his friends about it. Maybe over the course of a year, without meaning to, he embellished the story. People often exaggerate their exploits. Many a drunken spree gets wilder and better in the telling and retelling.

Did Derrek really need to go to a hospital? Shouldn't his friends have left him alone? Derrek's friends had also taken LSD. LSD can make people anxious, even paranoid. It's certainly possible that LSD clouded their judgment. Still, Derrek did appear to be going berserk. He could hardly expect his teenaged friends to remain calm while he ran around tearing his clothes off, screaming and laughing.

We're not going to pretend to you that after he woke up in the hospital Derrek learned his lesson and never took LSD again. Actually, he took it again several times. He even had one very bad trip where he spent several hours convinced he was in an "insane asylum." But it wasn't the bad trip that led him to give up LSD, though that certainly helped. Several trips turned out to be anticlimactic and repetitious. He simply grew bored with the drug.

LSD is certainly still around today. As we said, it's easy to concoct in home laboratories. It's popular mainly in circles that consider themselves "artistic." But it's not the big-deal drug it was back in the sixties. It seems that like Derrek, most people get bored with it after a while.

7

Coffee, Tea, and Speed

Throughout the world an enormous number of substances—from morning glory seeds to the latest laboratory concoctions with unpronounceable thirty-eight-letter names—have been used as drugs, to alter mood and perception. In the previous chapters we have covered those which are most important to teens today. But they are by no means the only drugs that you are likely to run into. Here—briefly—are some others.

The first one may surprise you.

Caffeine

Some people drink so much coffee you probably wouldn't recognize them if you saw them without a mug or cup in their hand. And being a teenager you've just got to know someone who drinks lots of soft drinks and cola. Maybe it's you who's hooked on coffee or cola. You probably never worried about it much. In our society coffee and cola are considered food. But they contain caffeine, and even in low to moderate doses caffeine is a strong drug. It's a stimulant that affects the central nervous system, the heart, blood pressure, metabolism, and the urinary bladder.

Caffeine was first isolated from coffee in 1921 and named in honor of the coffee plant, a shrub-like tree which originated in Ethiopia. When the tree's seeds (beans) are roasted they turn a rich dark brown and develop a delicious aroma. You probably think coffee's been around practically forever, but in historic terms it's a fairly recent drug, at least in our culture.

When Christopher Columbus was born, Europe was practically a drug-free environment, with one big exception: alcohol. Coffee and tea were not used. Tobacco was unknown. There were no hallucinogenic drugs to speak of, very little marijuana, very little opium, and no cocaine. Europeans wove alcohol into every fiber of their lives because alcohol was the only intoxicating drug they had. Europe passed on this legacy to the United States, and alcohol is still our foremost intoxicating drug. But the great geographic discoveries of Columbus and other explorers brought alcohol its first competition.

Columbus not only discovered America, he discovered tobacco. Coffee reached Europe via Arabia and Turkey and tea was brought from China, also in the seventeenth century. Europeans discovered the kola nut in West Africa. Coffee isn't the only source of natural caffeine. It's found in the kola nut, tea, several exotic plants, and in chocolate. Caffeine may be one of the reasons chocolate's so hard to resist.

Wherever coffee went, it usually provoked a strong negative reaction at first. When the Moslems of Arabia began using coffee in religious ceremonies the authorities reacted by prohibiting the drug. When coffee drinking continued to spread in Arabia people were punished, even beaten if they were discovered using it. But coffee caught on anyway and became fantastically popular in many Arab countries. Coffee was opposed in Europe at first, too, but it wasn't long before the drink was served in coffee houses where men met to discuss politics, read the newspapers, and enjoy their favorite brew. Some famous people became addicted to coffee. The great composer Johann Sebastian Bach loved coffee so much he composed the Coffee Cantata. The nineteenth-century French writer Honoré de Balzac was a notorious coffee addict. The coffee Balzac drank was so thick it was practically gummy. It gave him bad stomach cramps but he couldn't give it up. He just kept drinking more and more.

Coffee can make you jittery, give you insomnia and the shakes, and make you run to the bathroom. People who are coffee addicts or dependent on coffee get withdrawal symptoms in the form of headaches and restlessness when they're denied caffeine. Periodically, the medical profession issues warnings about coffee and what it may or may not do. Is there cause for alarm? We don't think so. Not until there's more definitive information, anyway. Besides, caffeine can be helpful. It's better to stop and have a cup of coffee on a long drive than risk cracking up the car. But that doesn't mean you should overdo caffeine. Don't sip coffee or chug-a-lug cola all the time. Try herbal teas, fruit juices, or seltzer water.

Pure caffeine is sometimes sold in pill form. One common brand is No-Doz. Teens sometimes take it when they have to study hard for an exam. It wakes up some people, doesn't affect others, and makes some people jittery. Stick to coffee or tea. They're quite potent enough. Sometimes caffeine is packaged to look like amphetamines and sold as a street drug for a very high price. But when it comes to street drugs you never know what you're getting. There's tons of fraud.

Glue Sniffing

The gas nitrous oxide was first synthesized in England in 1776. When inhaled it produced almost immediate intoxication. Usually the subjects began laughing uncontrollably —so the substance was popularly called "laughing gas." The "high" the gas gave, though it lasted only two or three minutes, was compared favorably with the effects of alcohol, and there was no hangover. The effect of nitrous oxide was so spectacular and so immediate that at public demonstrations crowds lined up and paid a small fee to experience the high or watch others act silly. For a while sniffing laughing gas for kicks became sort of a fad, particularly among students. But interest faded, and recreational use of laughing gas today is rare. Nitrous oxide is now used primarily by dentists as an anesthetic. In the musical *Little Shop of Horrors* the sadistic dentist gets his kicks from laughing gas, and finally accidentally kills himself with the gas.

Ether and chloroform—both powerful anesthetics—will produce intoxicating effects if inhaled. Ether has also been drunk, but generally only when traditional alcoholic products were unavailable. Ether and particularly chloroform can quickly render the user unconscious—sometimes permanently. They can also make the user feel pretty sick afterwards, and they have never enjoyed wide popularity.

There are a lot of household chemicals—varnish, lighter fluid, gasoline, and other petroleum products—whose fumes when inhaled will produce a sort of a giddy, drunken state. They can also produce nausea, vomiting, unconsciousness, and in extreme cases they can kill you.

Probably the greatest immediate danger from these substances, however, is that they are all extremely flammable, and even explosive. A stray spark, and it's all over.

Sniffing petroleum products produces a very low-quality

high, and is far more likely to make you sick than euphoric. Sometime quite young children will inhale gasoline or other fumes to get high, for the same reason that very young children will spin around and around until they get dizzy and sick. It's a new experience. But gasoline sniffing has never been considered a major social problem.

Glue sniffing, however, has been treated very differently. Inhaling the fumes from airplane glue will produce the same sort of short-term giddiness as the fumes from gasoline or paint thinner. There are also the same fairly remote, but possibly serious long-term dangers, and the immediate danger of fooling around with a highly flammable substance. But there is absolutely no indication that glue sniffing was a widespread phenomenon until 1959, when a series of sensationalized articles about the dangerous new "fad" appeared in newspapers in Denver, Colorado.

Pretty soon dire warnings about the disastrous physical and moral effects of glue sniffing were appearing throughout the country. One widely quoted authority maintained that glue-sniffing parties often led to heterosexual and homosexual orgies, and that "perverts" were luring children with the promise of glue fumes. The evidence for such statements was flimsy in the extreme.

Numerous deaths were attributed to glue sniffing. When closely investigated, however, there were only a small number of deaths, and in practically every one of these cases the victim had been sniffing glue with his head in an airtight plastic bag—and thus had died from asphyxiation, not glue fumes.

Laws against selling glue to minors were proposed and passed. A genuine glue-sniffing panic had been created among American parents.

What was the result of antiglue campaign? Before 1959 glue sniffing was essentially unknown among most teenagers. After the warnings, the raids, and the laws, somewhere from five to eight percent of graduating high school seniors had tried sniffing glue. So the campaign was not merely a failure, it was counterproductive. It created a menace where none had existed before. Kids were introduced to glue sniffing by being warned against it. A lot of them figured that if adults were so upset about the stuff it must be pretty good.

And even after the menace had been created, how serious was it? Not very. Except in rare cases glue sniffing is a foolish, but essentially harmless activity. It is far more likely to make you feel nauseated than high, and most kids get over the glue-sniffing phase very quickly.

Yet fear of the glue-sniffing menace remains strong. In 1986 the superintendent of a Texas school district proposed a policy of mandatory drug testing and complained:

"Over the years we've had one drug-awareness program after another in the schools. Nothing worked. I'm sick and tired of reading reports about kids wandering through school parking lots after sniffing glue."

Barbiturates and Other Downers

Barbiturates can calm a person down or put him to sleep. They have been used to treat epilepsy, and to ease convulsions, particularly in infants. They have also been used to treat high blood pressure, ulcers, and a variety of other conditions believed to be stress-related. They are in fact extremely useful drugs.

But tolerance to barbiturates builds quickly, and they can be addicting. Many authorities believe that the effects of barbiturate addiction are worse than those of alcoholism or morphine addiction. Withdrawal can be painful and dangerous. Perhaps the greatest danger of barbiturates is that it's easy to overdose on them, take too many—either accidentally or deliberately—and never wake up. They are among the most commonly used instruments of suicide, particularly for women.

Barbiturates were introduced into the U.S. in the early years of the twentieth century, and were widely prescribed by doctors—probably too widely prescribed.

The effects of barbiturates are very much like those of alcohol; in fact, barbiturates have sometimes been described as "solid alcohol." Taken in moderate doses barbiturates can sometimes induce a giddy state that is indistinguishable from being drunk. Why not just take a drink? Some people don't like to drink. As with the narcotic- and alcohol-laced tonics of an earlier era, barbiturates give the effect of booze without drinking.

In the mid-1940s, articles began to appear warning of the dangers of the nonmedical use of barbiturates—"thrill pills," they were called. It's difficult to determine if the scare stories about barbiturate "thrill pills" came in response to a real problem that had grown up underground, or if the scare stories helped to create the problem. Laws against nonprescribed barbiturates were passed, people were arrested, and a large illegal barbiturate market began.

In their book *Licit and Illicit Drugs,* the editors of *Consumer Reports* clearly believe that it was the scare that helped to create the problem:

"What might have been anticipated did in fact occur. Some people who would never for the world have taken a sedative or a sleeping pill now began getting drunk on the new 'thrill pills.' For them the warnings served as lure; illicit barbiturate use increased from year to year. Throughout the 1950s and 1960s, the relatively harmless sleeping tablets of the 1930s played their new role as one of the major illicit drugs in America."

At first barbiturates were used for recreational purposes by adults. Kids generally prefer stimulants to depressants. But word got around that you could get pretty drunk on "barbs." In the sixties the "downers" were among the most commonly used drugs among the teens and preteens. They could get the sleeping pills from their parents' medicine cabinet, and when that source dried up there was always the street dealer. At first most barbiturates were manufactured by the major drug companies. The companies were selling far more pills than the doctors were prescribing. As laws became more restrictive the pills began coming in from other countries, or were manufactured in back-alley labs.

As the barbiturates got a bad name, the pharmaceutical industry came out with a new line of drugs—the tranquilizers. These drugs are also known as the minor tranquilizers, to distinguish them from the really powerful drugs that are used to manage psychotic patients.

These drugs were first marketed in the fifties—just when the barbiturates were getting into trouble. They were advertised as chemicals that could make anxious and unhappy people feel relaxed and calm. The first of these products, with the trade name Miltown, became the best-known new drug of the fifties. And the public once again proved that practically any substance can be abused. Soon people were holding Miltown parties just to get high.

Other tranquilizers with names like Librium and Valium followed and have become part of American language and culture. If you want someone to cool off you might say, "Oh, go take a Valium." The tranquilizers are still among the most widely prescribed drugs in the world. Most of the users were women. Dad took a double scotch and water. Mom took Valium.

Though the tranquilizers were touted as being a radically

new development in the chemical control of moods, the effects are really not all that different from barbiturates, or even alcohol. They are somewhat less addictive, and don't make the user quite as drowsy. It's still not smart to try and drive while under the influence of tranquilizers. Withdrawal from tranquilizers is less painful than withdrawal from barbiturates or alcohol—but it's still no fun.

Tranquilizers have their place in helping some people cope with particularly stressful situations. But when the drugs are used to cope with the problems of everyday life, the result will be drug dependence. And there have been plenty of people who did become dangerously dependent on the tranquilizers prescribed by their doctors. As with so many new drugs, the problems showed up only after the drugs had been in use for a few years.

It was inevitable that the tranquilizers would also hit the streets. Generally they were taken for the same reasons that doctors prescribed them—to make people feel better and calmer. In addition the tranquilizers had the reputation of promoting sexual activity, which increased their popularity on the street. Like alcohol, they lower anxieties and inhibitions. But—also like alcohol—they can actually interfere with sexual performance.

All the warnings about the dangers of barbiturates must also be applied to tranquilizers. Don't be fooled by the fact that they are widely prescribed and might be found quite legally in your own home. Don't be misled by the *minor* tranquilizer label. They are powerful drugs. One is less likely to overdose on them than on barbiturates—but it can be done, and is done all the time. Tranquilizers are a favorite for suicides and attempted suicides. Accidental overdoses are depressingly common. Taking a few tranquilizers, and then taking a few drinks, has often proved to be a deadly combination. Don't ever do it.

It's seductively easy to slip into a dependence on tranquilizers. Even if you get them on the street they seem to be legitimate. You figure they're the same thing the doctor prescribes. They can make you feel less anxious, and help you sleep—in the short term. But you quickly develop a tolerance and have to keep upping the dosage in order to get the same effect. Then you're in trouble.

Fortunately the popularity of tranquilizers as a street drug appears to have declined considerably over the past few years. No one really knows why.

Amphetamines—Uppers

Nicknamed "uppers," amphetamines are synthetic stimulants which prove once again that a drug needn't be illegal to cause problems. Though amphetamines are rarely prescribed today, they were once abundantly produced in pill form by pharmaceutical companies, and doctors frequently gave them to patients who complained of being depressed or who wanted to lose weight. What was the result of all this pill popping? A lot of people added drug dependence to their list of troubles.

We generally think of amphetamines as being very modern, contemporary drugs, but amphetamine was first synthesized in 1887. It wasn't until 1927, however, that doctors first put amphetamine to work as a medication for the treatment of low blood pressure.

In 1932 plain amphetamine was marketed under the brand name Benzedrine. People who suffered from a rare disease called narcolepsy (an inability to stay awake) responded beautifully to the stimulating effects of Benzedrine. After Benzedrine came new compounds of amphetamines. Dextroamphetamine was marketed under the name Dexedrine, methamphetamine was marketed as Methedrine, and so on.

Drugs like methylphenidate were developed which differ in chemical structure from amphetamines but do essentially the same things.

Amphetamines, like cocaine, make people feel wide awake and alert, confident and elated. The euphoric effects of cocaine don't last long, while a single dose of amphetamine may last four hours or longer. Amphetamines are more dangerous than cocaine. The body simply can't handle them as well. But cocaine is a more treacherously seductive drug than amphetamines just because a high doesn't last as long. Users are constantly tempted to take more cocaine.

Amphetamines are generally used by people who need to stay alert for extremely long periods of time or who face an intense experience which requires a quick spurt of energy. As we indicated in our chapter on cocaine, long-distance truck drivers, athletes, dancers, actors, and students cramming for exams are among the groups who feel the lure of amphetamines.

Do amphetamines work? Some people don't respond to them at all. Others become frenzied and even disoriented when they take amphetamines. Some people use them for years without any problems by controlling the dose and allowing their bodies plenty of time to rest and recuperate from the drug's effects. But the drugs are potentially dangerous even for people who think they know what they're doing. The risk of becoming dependent on amphetamines is always there.

But even more basic, fatigue is a warning signal. Your body must have adequate sleep and rest to ward off illness and to function well. Cutting through fatigue with artificial stimulants is stupid and short-sighted. You only wear yourself out more. Even governments learned the hard way that for every high there's a low.

During World War II, American, British, German, and

Japanese troops were given amphetamines. Touted as a wonder drug that would eliminate fatigue and build strength, amphetamines turned out to be a disappointment and a mistake. Many soldiers who used them regularly became dependent on them or became so depressed after the euphoria faded that they weren't much good in combat. In the Soviet Union a select group of factory workers was given amphetamines to increase their productivity. But the workers responded so erratically to the amphetamines that the drugs were withdrawn and the program stopped. The drugs created more problems than they solved.

In the sixties amphetamines were often preferred over cocaine as a recreational drug. Heroin and amphetamine injections were popular, and some users not only took amphetamines but drank alcohol at the same time. Mixing amphetamines and alcohol is very dangerous. It can even prove fatal. When you read in the newspapers that somebody died of an overdose of amphetamines, check closely. You'll often discover that what really killed them was the combination of amphetamines and alcohol.

The sixties was also the era when a new breed of amphetamine user appeared on the scene, the speed freak. Speed freaks were usually teenagers or people in their early twenties who injected huge amounts of amphetamines intravenously. Speed turned healthy teenagers into emaciated wrecks (amphetamines are appetite suppressants) in weeks. Not only did speed freaks stop eating, they stopped sleeping. Speed freaks often became hysterical, crazed, violent, and paranoid, and were plagued by gruesome hallucinations.

Why would anybody become a speed freak? Some people loved the maniac high excessive use of stimulants brought them. Some people kept on injecting themselves with speed because coming down from such massive heights was horrible. Periodically speed freaks would crash into total exhaustion and severe depression, sleep for a couple of days, force themselves to eat something, then start the whole crazy suicidal binge all over again.

Speed freaks were so scary they alarmed the rest of the drug culture which, interestingly, began to police itself. The slogan "speed kills" caught on. People who used other kinds of drugs set out to actively dissuade potential drug users from trying speed. It worked. Many young people learned about the dangers of speed and kept away from it. Unfortunately, one negative aspect of amphetamines now being available primarily as a street drug is that it's harder to get amphetamines in pill form. Pills are the safest way to take amphetamines. The street version is generally powder, and that means users must snort or inject the drug.

Back in the fifties and sixties amphetamines in pill form were prescribed as tranquilizers even though amphetamines didn't make people very tranquil. They were mainly given to women, usually housewives who felt bored, tired, and unhappy. Amphetamines were supposed to cheer them up and energize them.

By and large the women weren't sick or in physical pain, so we have to ask ourselves precisely what the drugs were supposed to be treating. Amphetamines couldn't bring the women jobs, better relationships with their husbands, children, and friends, or real accomplishments that build self-esteem. Instead amphetamines were a kind of "happiness pill." What was being treated was life itself, with all its everyday problems and frustrations.

But there is no such thing as an innocent "happiness pill," and life is not a disease. Eventually physicians themselves came to realize that amphetamines didn't really help people face up to their problems and find solutions. All amphetamines did was to encourage people to escape into drug use when they felt overwhelmed by their problems, and this is the very essence of drug abuse. After a few years the situation changed and amphetamines could only be prescribed under limited conditions.

One final important point about amphetamines: Because they kill your appetite you may be tempted to use them to lose weight. Please don't. Even over-the-counter diet pills contain stimulants, and they really aren't good for you. We know how important looks are to teenagers. We know how much you want to be thin. But people who use diet pills often wind up like yo-yos, bounding up to fat and down to thin and up to fat and down to thin again without ever really learning how to keep weight off. Vicki's story may help you.

Vicki was thirteen and in the eighth grade. She wasn't fat but she was on the plump side. Still, every time Vicki looked in the mirror she felt she was seeing the winner of the "Miss Fat America" contest.

She was convinced that no boy (especially the gorgeous one in her math class) would ever like her because she was fat. She'd overheard kids calling her "that fat girl." Nothing she wore looked right. The fat was all in the wrong places anyways, around her hips and stomach instead of smacked up on her chest.

Vicki was desperate. She confided in her best friend Laura, who was thin, damn it. Laura let Vicki in on a little secret. She, Laura, took diet pills. She had several bottles at home which she'd happily give to Vicki.

Vicki took the bottles home and hid them in her room. She knew her parents would never approve of her taking any kind of pills except an occasional aspirin when she had her period or something prescribed by a doctor if she was sick.

For a few days Vicki got away with it. The diet pills did

kill her appetite and she skipped breakfast (claiming she was late for school) and barely touched lunch or dinner. Then her mother got suspicious and found the pills.

Her parents remained firm but they did listen. They decided that they had contributed to Vicki's problem. Cola and potato chips were always available to snack on in the house. Meals were large and usually followed by dessert.

Vicki's mother threw out the diet pills, pointing out that there was no way even to guess what the ingredients were. The bottles had no labels. You should never take other people's pills. That can be dangerous. But from now on the snacks disappeared from Vicki's home. There was more broiled chicken served, more fish and salads. Vicki drank skimmed milk, juice, and water instead of cola.

Controlling herself at school was hard. There was so much food around. Fortunately, most of the food in the school cafeteria tasted so awful Vicki wasn't wildly tempted to overeat. Exercise burns off calories, so she took dancing lessons and joined the track team. It was slow going at first, but at last Vicki shrank down to her dream size of seven. She kept her weight down, too. Because she'd achieved her goal on her own she felt proud of herself. She didn't need diet pills after all.

8

Steroids— "You Look Mahvelous!"

Let's imagine someone offered you a magic pill. The pill would allow you to get something that you very much wanted: perhaps the thing you wanted most in the world. But there's a catch. (There is always a catch in this sort of story.) The catch is that within five years the pill would kill you. Would you make that kind of a deal?

We're guessing that most of you would say, "No way! That's crazy. I've got a whole life ahead of me."

But there are young people who are not crazy but would give a very different answer.

There have been several surveys of top athletes, world-class runners, weight lifters, shot-putters, and the like. The basic question was, if you could take a pill that would make you an Olympic champion, but would kill you in one to five years, would you do it? In three different surveys, the majority of the athletes polled said yes!

Now you might figure the athletes don't really mean it. This magic pill business is all made up, so those who were surveyed don't take the question seriously. But you would

figure wrong. Athletes take the question very seriously indeed. For them there is a magic pill, or a magic drug—the
anabolic steroids. The steroids are not entirely magical.
They will not guarantee that the athlete who takes them
will die within five years, or indeed that the athlete will
suffer any long-term ill effects from the drug. But then they
don't guarantee that the athlete is going to win an Olympic
medal either.

As with all illegal drugs—and using steroids without a
doctor's prescription is illegal—the user becomes part of
an uncontrolled experiment in which he or she plays the
part of the guinea pig. This is particularly true of steroids,
because they are relatively new and powerful entries on
the drug scene. The long-term effects of steroids on large
numbers of people are still unknown.

World-class athletes are a very special group. Most of
them are extremely driven, even obsessed people. In order
to reach the level where an athlete can even think about
entering the Olympics, he or she must have put in years
of single-minded training. To the athlete the possibility of
winning the cherished medal, even at the risk of death,
might seem more attractive than it is to the average young
person. But steroids are not being offered only to athletes, though that is where their use began. The use of
steroids has now spread to the general population of young
people. Why?

You've probably seen the popular comedian Billy Crystal
do his "Fernando" routine. Fernando is the Latin celebrity
interviewer who is always saying to his guests "You look
mahvelous!" The comedian often ends his routine with the
line, "Remember, it's better to look mahvelous, than to feel
mahvelous." When Billy Crystal says it, it's a joke. But a
lot of people really feel that way—particularly teens. What
would you give, what kind of risks would you run, in order

to look marvelous? And the word is, at least for boys, that steroids can make you look marvelous.

Gary's Story

In high school Gary had been a star athlete, a pitcher on the baseball team and quarterback on the football team. Gary's high school wasn't one of those big power sports high schools, and while Gary was good he wasn't great. Still, he was one of the school's top athletes, and that gave him a lot of status. He never lacked for girlfriends. While he didn't have a Hollywood face, people told him he had a "good body." And all of that made Gary feel marvelous.

Then he went to college. He went to a large private university, but he didn't get an athletic scholarship. He hadn't expected one. He didn't harbor dreams of the NFL. Gary's major was engineering. Gary was realistic. But his introduction to college life was more of a shock than he expected.

He hadn't a hope of making the college football team, even though it wasn't a particularly good one. All of the varsity football players had been recruited with athletic scholarships, and they were all enormous. They made Gary, a normal-sized eighteen-year-old, feel like a skinny little dwarf. Even the baseball players were more skillful and much larger and stronger than he was.

Gary could have tried out for lacrosse or some other little-known college sport. But Gary had grown up playing football and baseball—these were the sports he knew, and he didn't want to change. He felt he was effectively cut out of college athletics. That hit him hard. He had never realized how much of his self-esteem was tied up with being thought of as an athlete. Needless to say his freshman year was an unhappy one.

Gary decided that over the summer he was going to "bulk up" through the use of exercise and steroids. He didn't figure that the drugs would get him on the football team. But if he couldn't be an athlete any more, he still wanted to look like one. He wanted people to think that he had a "good body" again.

Back at home in a small Connecticut town, Gary discovered that steroids were not that hard to come by. At the local gym some of the more active bodybuilders and weight lifters seemed to have easy access to the drugs. There was sort of a steroid underground that even had its own publications. One of the guys told Gary about a pharmacy where the steroids could be purchased, no questions asked. Another told him about a doctor in a nearby town who would write prescriptions for anyone. But there was an easier way to get the drugs. A fellow named Frank came around to the gym about three times a week, selling the stuff. Everybody seemed to know about it, and no one much cared. Some of the guys said that even the cops didn't care. A couple of cops worked out at the gym, and probably knew all about Frank. If Frank had been selling cocaine or other "real" drugs they would have busted him. Steroids weren't considered "real" drugs.

Some of Gary's friends from high school who had not left town had been working out at the gym regularly. They had been taking steroids for several months, and they looked great. They looked the way Gary wanted to look.

In the end he couldn't do it. But it wasn't the fear of the drug and its long-term effects that stopped him. It was the needle. The steroids Gary was offered were injectable. Gary couldn't stand the thought of sticking himself with a hypodermic needle. A couple of his well-meaning friends offered to do it for him—but that didn't help much. He worried about infections, he worried about AIDS. Though the needles he was offered were in sterile packages—no needle sharing, thus no AIDS danger—still he worried. He decided that he would try to stick to regular exercise, and learn to live with what nature gave him.

If he had been offered steroids in pill form (orally) the story might be different. It still may, for steroids are still a lure for Gary.

What are Steroids?

Anabolic steroids are synthetic derivatives of male sex hormones. The word anabolic refers to a substance that promotes growth and repair. Steroids is a term for the chemical compounds found in many organic substances, notably hormones. Doctors have known about anabolic steroids for a long time, and there are a lot of perfectly legitimate medical uses for them. They have, for example, been used after surgery to promote healing and reduce inflammation. They have also been used to aid in the treatment of bone diseases, and they can help to improve the condition of people, particularly the elderly, who have not been eating properly.

It's known that men are, in general, larger and physically stronger than women. It's believed that part of the difference in size and strength is due to differing hormone levels. The bodies of normal men and women contain both male and female hormones. But men have far higher levels of the male hormones. Thus it was logical to assume that if the level of male hormones in an individual were increased, this would also lead to an increase in size and strength.

A logical assumption—but not a safe one. The problem is that the chemical balance of the body is delicate and complex. Upset the balance by introducing something as powerful as synthetic male hormones—anabolic steroids

—and the results can be unexpected, and even disastrous, especially on the young. So while doctors knew about anabolic steroids, they were extremely reluctant to give them to people who were healthy. You can take chances to cure disease—otherwise, don't mess around with Mother Nature.

Still, not all doctors everywhere in the world were willing to adopt this cautious and conservative approach to the use of steroids. Some believe that the push to use steroids in athletics began in the Soviet Union and Eastern Europe.

During the late 1950s the Soviets and other Eastern European countries began to compete and win in international athletic competitions, including the Olympics. At about the same time the Soviets launched Sputnik—the first man-made earth satellite. It was a tough psychological blow for many Americans. That period inspired the U.S. space program, and it also inspired the development and use of anabolic steroids in athletics.

Dr. John Ziegler, one of the pioneers in the development of anabolic steroids, said:

"I felt the Russians were going to use sports as the biggest international publicity trick going . . . and strength sports especially . . . They saw it as a political advantage 100 percent."

So he began giving low doses of steroids to healthy athletes in the hope that it would help them beat the Russians. That was a decision he came to regret bitterly. Soon he found that other doctors were prescribing far higher dosages of steroids and that the athletes themselves were using the drugs in a completely unsupervised manner. "The athletes got their hands on the drugs in the 1960s, and in just fifteen to twenty-five years have turned it into one big mess," said Dr. Ziegler.

You might think that athletes would be the best examples

and strongest advocates of good health. They would want to build and preserve their bodies, not abuse them. And that's true, many athletes, perhaps most of them, are health fanatics.

But there is another side to athletes—a side that makes them excellent candidates for drug use. It is the single-minded desire to win. Athletic training is tough. Just going outside to play a little softball or tennis can make you feel good. To really train to compete at a high level is extremely difficult, and it can be painful. The higher the level at which the athlete competes, the more difficult and painful the training becomes.

Athletes have done all sorts of extreme things to their bodies in order to compete. Talk to anyone on your high school wrestling team and find out some of the things he had to go through in order to make the proper weight quickly. High school wrestlers have voluntarily starved and sweated to the point of passing out. Athletes are susceptible to a whole range of sometimes bizarre and dangerous diet and training fads. So sports isn't all good feeling, and it isn't all healthy.

Long before steroids came along there were drugs in athletics—not cocaine or other so-called recreational drugs used by some athletes off the field—but drugs used in the locker room to help athletes compete and win.

Where "Dope" Comes From

One of the most common words for drugs—dope—comes from athletic contests of a sort. It didn't mean stupid. The word *dop* was used by South African blacks to refer to a form of strong liquor that was commonly used. *Dop* was adapted by the Dutch-speaking Afrikaners as *dope,* and it was first used in Europe to describe a mixture of opium that was given to racehorses to make them run faster. The mixture first used on horses was quickly adopted by human athletes, and by the middle of the last century Dutch swimmers and cyclists were reportedly taking "dope."

By the start of the twentieth century athletes were trying a wide variety of ergogenic substances, that is, substances that are supposed to improve athletic performance. Some, like caffeine tablets, were relatively harmless—others could be deadly. In the 1904 Olympic games the American runner Tom Hicks nearly died after winning the marathon. It turned out Hicks had taken a large dose of strychnine and brandy before the race. Strychnine is a deadly poison, and Hicks wasn't the only athlete to use this potentially lethal combination.

But the real surge in drug taking among athletes came after World War II, with the introduction of amphetamines —speed. In Europe cyclists and speed skaters routinely took amphetamines—and freely admitted to it.

Around 1910 officials at racetracks got around to regularly testing horses for dope. Routinely testing athletes came later. After some highly publicized deaths and scandals, testing became fairly commonplace in world-class competition, particularly for amphetamines.

But amphetamines and other drugs known to be dangerous were not the only ones available to athletes. Painkillers and muscle relaxants were routinely administered to athletes to allow them to continue to play while they were injured—perhaps to play when they really shouldn't be playing. Anti-inflammatory drugs and drugs to promote healing—including some form of steroids—were also part of the medicine chest available to team physicians, trainers, and coaches. The entire professional and world-class sports world got used to the idea of taking injections and swallowing pills in order to compete. Not all of the drug taking was dangerous, wrong, or unethical. After all you'll routinely take a couple of aspirin tablets to get rid of a headache so you can perform better on today's algebra test. Nothing wrong with that. But the drugs being used in sports were far more powerful than a couple of aspirins. Frequent and accepted use of a variety of drugs in the locker room led to a climate in which drug taking seemed okay, so long as the result was performance and not pleasure.

Then along came the anabolic steroids. They seemed to have lots of advantages. In the first place they didn't appear to be immediately dangerous. Most athletes and team physicians knew of cases where people had simply dropped dead after taking amphetamines. That didn't happen if you took steroids—not as far as anyone knew. Not only were they relatively safe, they were also patriotic! Sure, there was a lot of grumbling publicly and privately about what the Soviets and their allies were doing with steroids. But instead of rejecting the whole notion of attempting to get the competitive edge through the use of hormones, the push was on to do it better than the Russians did. Finally, the anabolic steroids were legal in competition, at least at first. And when they became illegal they were still difficult to detect.

Do They Really Work?

There is a lot of controversy over whether the steroids actually do make athletes perform better. You might think the question of whether a drug works or not would be an easy one to answer, but it isn't. There is what scientists call the placebo effect. That means simply that if you take a drug that you genuinely and sincerely think is going to work, it probably will. The placebo effect has been tested repeatedly by scientists. Here's how.

Let's say you have a toothache. A doctor or someone else you trust and believe hands you a pill, and tells you it's a powerful painkiller. You take the pill and the pain subsides. The pill you were given, however, may only have been a sugar pill. There was nothing in it that should or could kill pain. It would be your belief in the pill, and the person who gave it to you, that killed the pain. That's the placebo effect. The placebo might not work on all people, but even powerful painkillers don't work on all people. Reactions to drugs or placebos are highly individual.

Sometimes placebos work as well as drugs designed for a particular task. The standard way of testing the effectiveness of a new drug is to give half the subjects in a test the real drug, the other half a placebo that looks like the real thing. If the drug works better than the placebo then it's assumed to be an effective drug.

The problem with testing anabolic steroids is that when they are used illegally it is at high and uncontrolled dosages. So some medical researchers believe that anabolic steroids simply don't help athletes. *The Physician's Desk Reference,* the book doctors most commonly consult to find out about drugs, states flatly, "Anabolic steroids do not enhance athletic ability."

But very few people involved with sports believe statements like that. A woman powerlifter interviewed for the TV program *20/20* complained that she had been told by the experts steroids don't work. Then she said she found out that they do work. After that she didn't believe anything she was ever told about steroids. So when she was told that steroids could have dangerous side effects she didn't believe that either. As it turned out, that time the experts were telling the truth.

Steroids are not going to turn an average athlete into an Olympic champion. But at the top level of competition they may give an athlete a slight edge. And that slight edge can be the difference between winning and finishing back in the pack. But at what cost? We'll get into the possible side effects of steroids shortly.

Though there can be argument over how effective steroids are in improving athletic performance, there is no argument over the fact that they do help an individual put on weight—and when combined with the proper kinds of exercise, muscle. Anyone can make his muscles bigger, and faster with steroids than without them.

When the authors were growing up, back in the 1950s, very few people did any intensive bodybuilding. Those who did were often considered strange and even creepy individuals. Now bodybuilding is extremely popular, even for women. Back in the fifties women bodybuilders were unthinkable.

Even more significant is that the bodies that are being built today are beyond the wildest dreams of the bodybuilders of twenty or thirty years ago. There was a fellow by the name of Charles Atlas who sold a widely advertised mail-order bodybuilding course based on what he called "dynamic tension." Ads with a picture of Atlas in a bathing suit must have appeared in every pulp magazine in the country. His physique was considered just about the ideal "body beautiful." Compared to today's bodybuilders Charles Atlas looks like a wimp. Many of today's women bodybuilders have more muscles than poor old Atlas.

The fashion for enormous, well-defined muscles has spread far beyond the circle of bodybuilders. Actors who were at one time considered well built suddenly appear on screen with enormous muscles. Is it all due to new workout techniques and equipment? Or is something else—anabolic steroids—involved?

Practically no one—bodybuilders or actors—will admit

to using steroids. Many openly denounce the use of such drugs. Can all of these denials be believed? There are plenty of well-known cases of athletes who denounced the use of drugs—one even made an antidrug commercial—shortly before being forced to enter drug treatment programs.

Some bodybuilding contests require tests for steroids. So do many major athletic events. In 1983 there was a big scandal at the Pan American Games in Venezuela. Fifteen athletes from ten different countries were disqualified after drug tests. Many others withdrew before competing when they discovered how sensitive the tests were to be. The tests could detect steroids used months earlier. But testing is not universal at athletic events, and it isn't always very effective. So the rumors of widespread steroid use among athletes continue.

Whether they got their physiques through the use of drugs or not, today's bodybuilders and beefcake actors have set a new standard of male good looks. Many high school boys dream of having the physique of an Arnold Schwarzeneger or Sylvester Stallone. If they can't get it through exercise—and there are distinct limits as to the sort of development that can be produced by even the most rigorous work on the Nautilus machine—then steroids seem like the answer.

Women athletes, particularly in the strength events like powerlifting, have used steroids. It is widely suspected that women bodybuilders do, too—though this is almost universally denied. As far as we can determine the use of steroids among women has not spread beyond athletics. A muscular look for women is more popular than it was ten or fifteen years ago. But the ideal look is still what can be produced by ordinary exercise—Jane Fonda, not a linebacker for the Jets. Steroids will produce a bulkier, far more "masculine" physique, than is considered attractive.

Still, the newly popular sport of women's bodybuilding may start a trend. Today's women bodybuilders are much more muscular than they were just a few years ago. There have been a lot of complaints that the women champs of today are "too masculine." Once again steroids have been hinted at, and hotly denied. But will a fashion for more massively muscled bodies among women set in, and will that lead to steroid use among teenage girls? Somehow we doubt it. And we certainly hope not. The danger of steroids to women, particularly young women, is far, far greater than it is to young men.

What's Wrong with Them?

A lot of people still don't think of anabolic steroids as "real" drugs, like amphetamines, cocaine, or even pot. The steroids don't change your mood. They make you look good —they sure don't make you feel good! Most users say you get a bloated and sluggish feeling from steroids. Some professional football players who used steroids to put on bulk then had to take amphetamines to regain their alertness for the game.

Sometimes steroids don't even make you look good. Many steroid users suddenly develop severe cases of acne. Here you are trying to look marvelous, and your new muscles are all covered with zits—not very attractive. Other users begin growing excessive body hair. Still others have reported that the drug makes them feel depressed or aggressive. These are short-term effects, which disappear when the steroids are discontinued.

The long-term effects of massive steroid use are not fully

known. But the data available to date is really scary—no kidding. The use of steroids has been linked to a variety of cancers, high blood pressure, kidney damage, strokes, heart attacks—a whole catalog of deadly diseases and conditions. You've got to remember that the steroids are powerful drugs that change the chemical balance of the whole body, often with unanticipated results.

These effects are slow to appear, however. Most steroid users argue that they will use the drugs for a limited period only, and thus avoid the most catastrophic results. Steroids, they point out, are not addictive like narcotics, or alcohol for that matter.

That's true as far as it goes. Steroids are not *physically* addictive. But the line between a physical addiction and emotional or psychological dependence on a drug is a very thin one, and in practice it often makes no difference at all whether you are addicted or simply dependent. If you feel the steroids have given you the body you want—the body you have always wanted—then it's tough to stop. Drop the drugs and you suddenly don't look like Superman any more. You have to work harder in the gym to maintain the muscles and often no matter how hard you work you can't do it without the drugs. You get flabby. So you put up with the discomfort, and push the long-term dangers to the back of your mind. Nothing will happen for years, you tell yourself, and besides, I can stop any time I want. Except that you can't.

Another common rationale says that at least these drugs are "legal" even if they are obtained and used illegally, without the proper prescription or medical supervision. They are not truly street drugs. Even this is not necessarily true. A lot of the steroids being sold under the counter are look-alike copies of products made by reputable drug companies. That is, they come in properly marked and labeled bottles and weren't cooked up in some unsanitary backwoods laboratory. But many of these drugs come from countries where the regulations about what drugs can be sold and used are far looser than they are in the U.S. And some of the drugs are simply counterfeit. The drugs are put in bottles that look like those available in the U.S. but aren't. Some of these drugs would not be legal anywhere.

Until recently the U.S. government took a pretty lenient attitude toward smuggling steroids across the border. The kid caught bringing in a few joints from Mexico could wind up in jail. The coach or trainer smuggling in a trunkload of illegal steroids might avoid prosecution entirely. However, as the dangers of steroids have become more obvious, and their use more widespread, the authorities have begun cracking down. Recently a group including a couple of prominent athletes and coaches was arrested for smuggling steroids. They now face serious jail time. So the government's easygoing acceptance of steroids is changing. Yet there is no reason to believe that so long as the demand exists, the drugs won't continue to be brought across the borders. Heroin, cocaine, and marijuana flow with ease into the U.S., despite repeated government crackdowns and seemingly endless "wars on drugs."

If you take steroids obtained on the black market you must realize that they are like any other street drug. You don't really know where they came from, or what they contain.

A Bad Example
In his book on steroids and other drugs used by athletes, *Death in the Locker Room,* Dr. Bob Goldman described the

incident that first got him involved in research on the effects of steroids. It was the death of a friend and former idol, a man that he called John.

Dr. Goldman says John was the "holder of a major world title, dozens of lesser titles, and had been a football star." John was a role model for a lot of the kids who came to his health club, and it was a position he took very seriously. He was in Dr. Goldman's words, "a truly good man."

He also took drugs—anabolic steroids. John was in his thirties, and competitively over the hill, but he wanted desperately to retain that body he had worked so hard for. Despite suspicions about the dangers of steroids, John didn't really see anything wrong with them. A lot of the guys were taking them.

After about three years of steroid use John got sick, and his diagnosis was a rare form of kidney tumor that has been linked to the use of steroids. By the time the tumor was found it was really too late to do anything. Chemotherapy only prolonged John's life for some six months. The treatment also had terrible side effects, including almost constant nausea.

Writes Dr. Goldman: "In retrospect I judged it a supreme irony that John told me he had heard that smoking marijuana might prevent the terrible nausea that accompanied his chemotherapy, but that he didn't want to do it because it might get back to the kids, and he didn't want to set a bad example."

This story illustrates one of the main reasons we think steroids are so dangerous for today's teens. People still don't think of them as being "real" drugs. You've already heard plenty about the dangers of heroin, cocaine, even marijuana. Because steroids are supposed to make you look marvelous rather than feel marvelous, they are not considered quite so immoral, or quite so dangerous. Steroid use is still encouraged by some coaches and trainers, and even a few parents with their heads full of dreams of athletic glory for their boy. These same people would be horrified by someone pushing coke to young athletes.

Another reason that steroids are so dangerous is that their forms are constantly changing. Since they are produced in the laboratory, there always seems to be a new wonder compound available. One of the drugs that has been getting a lot of publicity recently is the Human Growth Hormone, or HGH. Hormones that regulate human growth have been known since the 1920s, and they have sometimes been given to children who might otherwise have been extremely small. But naturally produced HGH was hard to obtain and very, very expensive. There was never enough to go around even in legitimate medical treatment.

During the 1980s it became possible to produce synthetic HGH in the lab. It's not easy, and the drug is still extremely expensive, but there is now enough of it available to be misused.

HGH can apparently produce impressive gains in size and bulk—and some frightening side effects. In addition to all of the other problems that a user can get from steroids, HGH can also produce the condition known as acromegaly. In acromegaly the face and jaw are excessively and permanently elongated. There is a growth of the brow ridges and the facial features become thick and heavy. Bones of the hands and feet soon become outsized. It is what Dr. Goldman calls "the Frankenstein syndrome." The condition is irreversible.

Acromegaly occurs among people who have a serious disorder of the pituitary gland, which produces the human growth hormone. The results can be so extreme that in an earlier era victims of the condition might wind up in freak shows. Whether use of synthetic HGH will produce such extreme cases is unknown. But do you know anybody who wants to find out?

Drugs like cocaine and heroin have been around a long time. The dangers are known, even if they are not fully appreciated. But steroids are new. And because they are not psychoactive and not physically addictive we still feel that they are not so bad. This attitude is wrong, foolish, and dangerous.

Perhaps some day anabolic steroids will serve some useful purpose for athletes, or just ordinary well people— perhaps. But that day isn't now and it may be never. If you use them now you have signed up for the role of human guinea pig.

9

How Drugs Became Illegal

If a nineteenth-century American could suddenly be transported to modern-day America he or she would be puzzled by a lot of things. Airplanes, television, superhighways, rock music are developments that would not only have been unknown a century ago, but barely hinted at. The time traveler would understand the language well enough, but would have a lot of trouble understanding modern attitudes in politics, personal relations, and drugs. The attitude toward drugs would be very puzzling indeed.

If nineteenth-century America wasn't exactly a "Dope Fiend's Paradise," as it has sometimes been called, respectable folk were a lot more worried about whiskey than cocaine. One hundred years ago a drugstore was a real *drug* store. If you had a cough you could go down to the corner drugstore for a bottle of the ever popular Mrs. Wilson's Soothing Syrup. The syrup was very soothing because it contained a heavy dose of morphine. Syrups of this type were commonly sold to mothers to ease "colic" or teething pain in infants. The infants were not merely soothed—they were completely knocked out.

In addition to the enormous number of drug-laced over-the-counter preparations or patent medicines, doctors themselves regularly prescribed far more powerful compounds for the relief of pain, to produce sleep, to calm anxieties, to ease the symptoms of an enormous range of illnesses.

The dangers of drugs containing heavy doses of morphine and cocaine were well known to doctors, even if the regular consumer of Mrs. Wilson's Soothing Syrup didn't quite understand why the stuff worked. Doctors often prescribed large doses of drugs they knew to be addicting to patients, particularly those who suffered from chronic and severe pain, because the doctors didn't know what else to do. There was simply no other effective treatment available. Doctors did not consider addiction the worst possible fate.

The opium-laced patent medicines were not manufactured in back alleys or by foreign criminals. They were made and sold by very respectable American businessmen. When suggestions were made that perhaps such concoctions were dangerous, and should be regulated, the businessmen held up the banner of free enterprise, cried no government interference, and generally carried the day.

Drinks for Men, Drugs for Women

The majority of those who took drug-laced patent medicines were women. These medicines were often recommended for "female troubles," a vague term which could mean anything from menstrual cramps to depression. One suspects that the real reason women took drugs more frequently than men is that in the nineteenth century drinking by women was still frowned upon. Men went to the saloon and drank their troubles away. Women went to the drustore and then downed their narcotic "medicines" or "tonics" at home.

There certainly were a lot of people who were dependent on drugs. Flipping through nineteenth-century publications you can find ads for opium-laced patent medicines side by side with advertisements for one or another quack cure for morphine addiction.

While taking drugs, and certainly becoming addicted to them, was not considered desirable or even socially acceptable, the reaction in the nineteenth century was far different than it is today. Dr. Watson surely did not approve of his friend Sherlock Holmes's cocaine habit, but he wasn't horrified, nor were the millions of respectable middle-class readers of the great detective's adventures. They felt about Sherlock Holmes's cocaine much the same way a later generation of readers felt about another fictional detective, Sam Spade's heavy drinking—it was an allowable, almost an attractive vice.

In the nineteenth century drug use was considered a far less serious problem than alcoholism. A common treatment for alcoholics was to turn them into morphine addicts. In 1889 Dr. J. R. Black wrote a widely read article called "Advantages of Substituting the Morphia Habit for the Incurably Alcoholic." Morphine, he wrote, "is less inimical to healthy life than alcohol." It "calms in place of exciting the baser passions and hence is less productive of acts of violence and crime; in short ... the use of morphine in place of alcohol is but a choice of evils, and by far the lesser...."

Dr. Black became practically poetic:

"The mayors and police courts would almost languish for lack of business; the criminal dockets with their attendant legal functionaries would have much less to do than they now have—to the profit and well-being of the community. I might, had I time and space, enlarge by statistics to prove the law abiding qualities of opium-eating peoples, but of this anyone can perceive somewhat for himself, if he carefully watches and reflects on the quiet, introspective gaze of the morphine habitué and compares it with the riotous devil-may-care leer of the drunkard."

So late twentieth-century America's eternal "war on drugs" would be very puzzling to the visitor from the nineteenth century. In that era drugs were no big deal. If they were a problem they were primarily a medical problem, not a social or moral one. People took drugs for medical reasons —even if that reason was simply to cure depression. Except for a few "artists" and "foreigners," people in America didn't take drugs to get high. If you wanted to get high you got drunk.

The energies that are today directed against pot, cocaine, and heroin were then directed against "the demon rum." By the end of the nineteenth century there was a strong prohibitionist tide running in the country.

We do not mean to imply that people were totally unconcerned about drugs and their effects. By the turn of the century there were an estimated 200,000 addicts in the United States. Most of the addiction resulted from taking the medicines of the day, either patent medicines or prescription drugs.

The attack on the free and easy use of drugs was led by the crusading journalists called "muckrakers." In a landmark series of articles that appeared in the magazine *Colliers* in 1905, Samuel Hopkins Adams attacked the entire patent medicine field. He was most bitter toward the manufacturers of "catarra powders" that contained cocaine and soothing syrups that contained opium. It was a "shameful trade," he asserted, "that stupefies helpless babies and makes criminals of our young men and harlots of our young women."

The patent medicine manufacturers raised their usual (and usually successful) cry of free enterprise, but by 1905,

the mood of the country had changed. Federal regulation
of manufacturing had begun, and among the first pieces of
regulatory legislation passed was the Pure Food and Drug
Act of 1906. This act required that medicines containing
opiates and certain other drugs be clearly identified on the
label. Later amendments required that the quantity of each
drug be stated, and that the purity of each drug meet official
standards. If you wanted to take drugs in patent medicines,
at least you should know what you were getting.

As yet there was no mass movement in the U.S. to ban
all drugs, as there was to ban all alcohol. But in 1914 Congress passed the Harrison Narcotic Control Act. It was a
curious bill, really sort of an afterthought. There had been
a number of international conferences on drug trafficking
—particularly in the Orient. Wars had been fought in China
over who was to control the opium trade. The Harrison bill
was seen primarily as means of fulfilling certain international obligations to control the drug trade. It appeared to
be a bill that would regulate the sale of opium and cocaine
(wrongly described as a narcotic). The drugs were to be
confined to the doctor, dentist, or veterinary surgeon who
could dispense them "in the course of his professional
practice only." At the time not many thought of it as a bill
that would rapidly make opium products and cocaine illegal for those who needed and wanted them most. However, the most active supporters of the bill were ardent
prohibitionists. They may have looked upon the Harrison
Narcotic Control Act as setting a precedent for banning
alcohol.

Since drug addiction wasn't defined as a disease, doctors
who dispensed drugs to addicts simply to maintain their
addiction were considered to be breaking the law. Those
who did were quickly arrested, tried, convicted, and some
imprisoned. Doctors soon learned that to try to give drugs

to addicts, even those who were leading relatively stable and useful lives, was to court professional disaster. Whether this is what those who framed the bill had intended is not clear. But it's what happened. Very quickly all legitimate sources for opium products and cocaine disappeared.

The addicts, however, did not disappear. There were still hundreds of thousands of them out there—and they were desperate. Some signed themselves into hospitals and sanatoriums to try and kick their habits. Treatments for the truly addicted were no more successful seventy years ago than they are today—that is to say not very successful at all. The majority of addicts turned to other sources for their drugs—other sources are always available. And so began the mass criminalization of drugs in the United States.

Within a half dozen years after the passage of the Harrison Act, Prohibition—a ban on all alcoholic beverages—became the law of the land. Prohibition was from the start an unmitigated disaster. Though the total number of alcoholics in the U.S. may have fallen slightly during the Prohibition era, most people kept right on drinking. The liquor was more expensive, often dangerously adulterated, and supplied by criminals who became rich and powerful, corrupted law enforcement officials and politicians, and killed one another in disputes over territory and money. The government spent an enormous amount of time and taxpayers' money in an attempt to stop the illegal liquor trade—but no matter how many bootleggers were thrown in jail, no matter how many illegal liquor shipments were smashed, it made not the slightest dent in the booze trade. After thirteen years, "the noble experiment," which is what Prohibition was called, was declared a failure and abandoned. Today, when practically everyone recognizes the enormous social problems brought on by drinking (far worse than any social problems created by drugs) there is no serious effort to bring back Prohibition.

The Harrison Act, which banned drugs, was really no more successful than the Volstead Act, which banned liquor. Though the total number of addicts appears to have been reduced somewhat, the condition of the vast majority that remained had become infinitely more wretched. Within a few years a large criminal enterprise had grown up to supply the illegal drugs to those who craved them, of course at much higher prices. An editorial in *American Medicine* reported:

"One only has to think of the stress under which the addict lives, and to recall his lack of funds, to realize the extent to which these ... afflicted individuals are under the control of the worst elements of society."

Since the Harrison Act had turned all addicts into criminals, it created a new type of criminal addict—the individual who stole, or became a prostitute in order to support his or her habit. The image of the drug taken began to change: instead of the "introspective" morphine addict, there was the crazed "drug fiend."

Practically everyone agreed that the Harrison Act, like the Volstead Act, wasn't working as it was supposed to, yet there was virtually no attempt to repeal or fundamentally alter the legislation. In 1918 the first of a seemingly endless line of congressional committees was set up to examine all the problems the act had created. The committee acknowledged that the drug problem had actually gotten worse since the act was passed, but recommended only that the Harrison Act be enforced more strictly than ever.

Since that time the history of attempts to control the use of drugs in this country is a bit like a movie that is endlessly being remade, with only slight variations in plot and character. The ending always comes out the same, and the ending is not a happy one.

Fashions in Drugs

Though the attempts to control drugs have a depressing similarity, the drug scene itself is constantly changing. Take marijuana, certainly the drug of choice (after beer) for the American teenager. Though the effects of marijuana have been known for centuries, and it is widely used throughout the world, it was practically unknown in America until the 1920s. During the Prohibition era, the price of alcohol went up and people went looking for new ways of getting high. One of them was marijuana. At that time the laws controlling marijuana were local and loose. In some areas there were no laws at all. In other areas penalties for use were fairly severe. After Prohibition was repealed public interest in marijuana began to drop off. But the man who was in charge of enforcing drug laws in the U.S., Commissioner Harry J. Anslinger, did not lose interest. He lobbied hard for federal antimarijuana legislation, and by 1937 Congress had passed a Marijuana Act, modeled on the Harrison Act. For all practical purposes marijuana became illegal everywhere in the country.

Marijuana use remained at a fairly low level throughout the forties and fifties, except in certain communities. It was more widely used among Hispanics, for example. Some of the anti-marijuana agitation had more than a hint of anti-Hispanic bigotry to it. It was also used by jazz musicians and others whose lifestyles were considered unconventional.

The authors, who grew up during the fifties, first heard

of marijuana through the statements and literature issued
by Commissioner Anslinger's office. We were warned about
it pretty regularly, though no one we knew ever smoked
the stuff, or had even seen it. No one believed the warnings
and we suspect that if we could have gotten our hands on
marijuana we would probably have tried it, just because
we had heard so many unbelievable warnings.

The explosive growth in the use of marijuana in the U.S.
came in the sixties—ironically after many years of antimarijuana agitation from the government. The hippies and
rock music were widely blamed for this new popularity of
pot. True enough, the smell of marijuana hung heavy over
the famous Woodstock festival, and most other rock con-
certs. But a lot of young Americans were first introduced
to marijuana while serving in Vietnam. Pot smoking was a
way to deaden the terrors and boredom of war. When the
veterans returned to the U.S. they brought the habit back
with them.

The legal response to marijuana varied from place to
place and time to time. Though marijuana was essentially
illegal everywhere in the U.S., in many places the law
was simply ignored, even by the police. In other places
marijuana use was pursued aggressively by the authorities.
Possession of even a few joints could result in a stiff jail
sentence.

The sixties also saw the introduction of the psychoactive
drugs—particularly LSD. After a brief honeymoon with public
opinion, LSD soon replaced even heroin in the public's
perception as the most dangerous drug. The press was filled
with exaggerated and often totally untrue stories of the
horrors of the drug. These were reactions to the exaggerated and often totally untrue stories of the glories of the
drug which had appeared earlier.

Drugs do not exist in a vacuum. People's attitudes toward them are shaped by a lot more than medical facts. LSD, while it has its dangers, is nonaddicting, and ultimately boring. Most people were not reacting to the drug itself, but to the lifestyle it appeared to promote. Parents were terrified that their own children were rejecting their values, rejecting everything they had worked for, for themselves and their children. Drugs like LSD that seemed to bend the mind and change the personality were blamed.

Another Medical Mistake

With drugs there is a depressing tendency for history to repeat itself. In the late nineteenth century doctors too freely prescribed opiates for whatever ailed you, from severe pain to anxiety. In the fifties and sixties the same pattern developed with stimulants like amphetamines (uppers) and the barbiturates and other tranquilizers (downers). It's almost scary to compare the late-nineteenth-century ads for the wonders of opium-laced syrups and tonics with the mid-twentieth-century ads for stimulants and tranquilizers. Pharmaceutical companies advertised these highly profitable drugs as cures for many of life's stresses and disappointments. The advertising was done only in medical journals, but doctors began prescribing them in quantity. The public heard all about the drugs and began asking for them, demanding them from doctors. While amphetamines and tranquilizers do have legitimate medical uses, they were clearly overused.

It's impossible to know how much of an effect the sight of mom and dad popping pills to go to sleep, to get up, to get energy and to calm down affected the kids of the sixties. But the uppers and the downers, under a variety of names, soon hit the streets. They either reached the black market from legitimate drug companies or were manufactured in back-alley laboratories.

These drugs can be extremely powerful, and extremely dangerous. We don't mean to imply that their use was ever encouraged or even tolerated by American society in general. But somehow they never provoked the sort of horror that accompanied far-less-potent marijuana and LSD. Perhaps that is because a lot of adults were already familiar with them.

The street use of amphetamines, particularly in its injectable form, speed, declined—not so much because of any governmental, educational, or medical campaign against the drug, but primarily because the dangers became obvious to the drug-using population. The teenage drug users weren't convinced by "experts" they didn't believe anyway —they saw what the drug could do to their friends, and it scared them. But as the use of amphetamines declined, the popularity of cocaine rose once again.

The Situation Today

Organized crime does not issue regular reports on drug sales, so drug use can only be determined indirectly. Most of the statistics are obtained by surveys—simply asking people if they have used drugs recently. That may be an accurate measure of drug usage, or simply a measure of how willing people are to admit they have used drugs. But if we accept the statistics, then it appears that the casual use of marijuana and many other drugs has been in decline since the early seventies. Does that mean the hard-line antidrug approach is working?

There are several facts which make that conclusion questionable. First, the level of cocaine use has risen dramatically. Its use has spread from the affluent to the poor (the reverse of the usual trend in drug use). Moreover, consumption of alcohol, which has always been the drug of choice, remains high among teens and those of college age.

It's safe to predict that the use of cocaine, particularly in the form of crack, will also begin to decline. This will be brought about not so much by information campaigns or the arrest of crack dealers. As the users themselves see the serious consequences the drug has on their friends, they may begin to give up the drug. It's easier to give up crack than to give up heroin. A lot of lives will be shattered, but the crack epidemic will subside. That's what happened with speed.

But will cocaine then be replaced by some new drug, or perhaps increased consumption of alcohol? As we have said there are always changing fashions in drugs. It has happened before.

Drugs and AIDS

Fear and hatred of drugs and drug users tends to overwhelm any attempts to think about the subject rationally. A glaring and really horrifying example is the subject of drugs and the deadly disease AIDS. AIDS has reached epidemic proportions among intravenous (IV) drug users. IV drug users very often share needles, and the needles they use are almost never sterilized. If one IV drug user who carries the deadly virus in his bloodstream shares his needle with another user, he is likely to spread the disease. A small amount of blood—containing the virus—will remain on the needle. It will then be injected directly into the bloodstream of the second user.

In the U.S. you can't buy clean hypodermic needles

without a prescription. The only people who would want needles besides those who are taking medically approved drugs would be illegal drug users. Since government officials didn't want to give the appearance of approving drug taking in any way, the sale of needles that would be used by IV drug users has been banned. The sale of certain sorts of pipes and other drug paraphernalia is also illegal in many parts of the country.

But in the face of the AIDS threat there were tentative suggestions that addicts be supplied with clean needles. The needles wouldn't cure the addiction, but at least the possibility of being infected with a deadly disease and infecting others would be reduced. No one knew if the distribution of clean needles would really work. In general IV drug users are pretty self-destructive. They might simply ignore the clean needles and go on using drugs in the same old way. But it seemed worth trying.

Yet suggestions that needle distribution be tested were met with hostility and outrage. People said not only that needle distribution wouldn't work, but that it was morally wrong to give addicts anything that would allow them to carry on their addiction; even if the alternative was a deadly disease. In most places in the U.S. it is political suicide for an elected official to advocate the distribution of clean needles to addicts.

That doesn't make any sense. Withholding needles won't cure anyone's addiction. No one is going to become an IV drug user simply because he or she can get a free needle. But the fear and hatred is so intense that it has, so far, overwhelmed even a modest attempt to curb the spread of a deadly disease.

There has also been no real move to increase the number of methadone maintenance programs, which are already overcrowded. Methadone, which is drunk, gets people off heroin, which is injected.

Only the Mob Is Happy

No one, with the possible exception of the organized crime bosses who sell illegal drugs, is satisfied with the way the drug problem has been handled in the U.S. While the total percentage of addicts has probably declined somewhat since the Harrison Narcotic Control Act was first passed in 1914, the addicts have not gone away. Because they must buy their drugs from an illegal source, and probably finance their habits by illegal means, they are a far worse threat to themselves, and to society at large, than the pre-1914 addicts.

There are endless announcements of drug seizures at the border, or of the arrest of this or that organized crime drug kingpin. The jails are filled with drug takers and sellers. The phrase "the killings were drug-related" seems to be part of half the crime stories on the evening news. The "war on drugs" costs millions every year, and there are constant demands that more—much more—be spent. Yet no one seriously believes that the illegal drug trade will be stopped or even slowed significantly, no matter how much money is spent, so long as the demand for drugs remains high. Drugs make millionaires out of criminals today just as illegal booze made millionaires out of criminals during Prohibition. Drug money finances vast corruption in the U.S. and foreign countries. A couple of small, poor nations are virtually controlled by drug producers and smugglers who supply the drug market in America.

As we said, practically everyone would agree that the attempts to control drugs since 1914 have been a dismal failure. And no one really knows what to do about it.

Perhaps the Harrison Narcotic Control Act and all that followed was a basic mistake. Perhaps drugs should never have been made totally illegal. Could things be worse than they are today?

It's impossible to say with any certainty, of course, but they might be. If drugs were available freely and legally there would almost certainly be more addicts, more abusers. Sure, they wouldn't be criminals anymore, but most alcoholics aren't criminals either. That doesn't mean alcoholism isn't a problem for the alcoholic and all who are close to him or her.

Drinking is a disaster for a certain percentage of people, but so many people in America do drink that it has proved impossible to ban alcohol. Smoking is also a tremendous health hazard, but smoking too is so deeply ingrained in our society that it would be impossible to ban tobacco effectively. Education has reduced the number of smokers, and that's the best we can hope for.

Drugs are different. Most people in our society don't do drugs. Or they use them so infrequently that illegality is not something that bothers them very much.

It's been argued that pot and even cocaine are not as physically destructive as alcohol, or nearly as addictive as nicotine. Those arguments may be correct. But they don't make any difference in the real world.

Every society has those drugs that it accepts and calls legal, and those drugs it does not accept and deems illegal. A few years ago there were a fair number of people in the U.S.—not a majority, but a substantial minority—who favored the legalization or at least the decriminalization of marijuana. Even there, however, public opinion has turned around. The number of people favoring marijuana legalization has dropped. We suspect that a lot of people who use marijuana occasionally don't want it legalized. As far

as cocaine or other drugs—sentiment against any loos-
ening of drug laws is absolutely overwhelming.

There may be some ebb and flow in the way laws are
enforced. But there is no reason to believe that there is
going to be any major change in U.S. drug laws or public
attitudes.

That's just how it is.

10

Testing, One, Two, Three

It's two o'clock in the afternoon on a perfectly ordinary school day. Suddenly the principal's voice comes booming over the loud speaker. "Attention, attention. All classes will be prepared for testing." He's not talking about the SATs —he's talking about the mandatory drug tests.

You had heard that the school was supposed to start a program of drug testing for every student, but since you don't take drugs, you weren't worried. There had been some arguments at the school board, but the students were never really consulted. You didn't think much about the program. Finally the tests are here, and the announcement has come as a surprise. It had to be a surprise, otherwise the tests wouldn't be any good in detecting those who were on drugs.

Boys and girls are separated and told to line up, a class at a time, outside of their respective bathrooms. Then each student is carefully searched. In other schools there had been incidents of students who were worried about being caught by the tests carrying samples of "clean" urine to substitute for their own. The English teacher looks nervous and embarrassed as he asks you to turn out your pockets and then frisks you.

You are then handed a small bottle and told to fill it up. You must urinate in the bottle under the watchful eye of a couple of other teachers who are monitoring the test. That's another guard against cheating. What if you borrowed someone else's urine, or added some chemical, or simply filled the bottle up with tap water? That would defeat the whole purpose of the test.

Among the boys there is a lot of macho joking. But the jokes cover a lot of nervousness. A couple of the guys are so nervous they can't pee, particularly with the goofy chemistry teacher watching them. It's terribly embarrassing. Finally they're sent out to drink some water and told to come back and try again. Some guys have to wait around for hours.

The test is even worse and more embarrassing for the girls. One of the more outspoken and rebellious girls refuses flat out to give a urine sample. "What are you looking at?" she shouts out at a teacher monitoring the tests. The girl is taken off to the principal's office. To refuse to take the test means immediate suspension. You go to a quiet, law-abiding school, so most students go through with the test, even if they don't like it.

When each bottle is filled, it is labeled and sealed, and put in a rack for shipment to the testing laboratory. Results, you are told, will be back in about two weeks.

All the way home you worry. Okay, so you smoked a joint a couple of months ago. Would a urine test be able to pick that up? Nahh, they're not that sensitive. Or are they? Didn't you hear that sesame seeds make drug tests turn out positive? Weren't those sesame seeds you had on a bagel yesterday? How about those pills the doctor gave you for your sinuses? What if there's a mistake? What if the samples get mixed up? Half the time the school can't keep your grades straight—how are they going to handle all those bottles?

And what about the laboratory where the testing is done? How careful and accurate are they going to be? Your uncle Bill works in one of those testing laboratories, and your uncle Bill is an idiot. Who but a bunch of idiots would spend their days testing urine anyway? Some joker may mix up the results just for the hell of it.

What happens if the test comes back positive? Will anyone believe that you're not on drugs? It'll go on your school record and follow you the rest of your life. There goes any chance for a good college or a scholarship. Who wants a druggie, anyway? Drugs are illegal, so the police will be told. "Honest, officer, it's a mistake, somebody must have mixed up the bottles." "Yeh, sure, kid, they all say that."

You get home late. Your mother is waiting for you. She's already heard about the tests at the school. "Everything alright, honey?" she asks. "You're not worried, are you?"

"No, I'm not worried. I've got nothing to worry about." But you look worried, and now your mother is worried too. And suspicious.

It's been an awful and degrading afternoon and it's going to be a tough two weeks of waiting.

That little scene may not have taken place anywhere in America yet. It may never take place in public schools in America. But mass drug testing or screening of all high school students has been seriously proposed by some powerful politicians. A few school districts throughout the country have tried to start mass testing programs. Some private schools may use drug tests as an entrance requirement. Drug testing is a subject that has been talked about a great deal and certainly is going to be discussed again. You should know something about it. After all, you're the one who may be most directly affected.

How Do Tests Work?

Whenever you swallow, inhale, or inject any substance, it doesn't just disappear into your body. Traces of it may remain detectable in your cells, your blood, your urine, even your breath for hours, days, weeks, or months.

The most familiar form of substance abuse test in use in the United States today is the so-called Breathalyzer test. That's the test that highway patrolmen give to drivers they have stopped and who they suspect are drunk. The driver is asked to breathe into a plastic bag. Chemical crystals in the bag turn a telltale color if they come in contact with a predetermined level of alcohol in the breath. The Breathalyzer test is rarely given randomly. That is, the police don't stop everybody on the highway and make them take a Breathalyzer test. If the police see a car that is being driven erratically, or have some other reason to believe that the driver may have been drinking, they then administer the test. Anyone can refuse to take a Breathalyzer test, but if they do they may wind up in jail.

A more accurate measure of the number of drinks a person has had comes from a blood test. The amount or level of alcohol in a person's system can be determined by laboratory examination of a small sample of the person's blood. In many states if you have as little as .05 percent alcohol in your blood you are considered drunk.

The most common method of testing for drug use is by

laboratory examination of a person's urine. There are a large number of different sorts of urine tests that can be used to detect a tremendous array of drugs: barbiturates, amphetamines, opiates, cocaine, PCP, marijuana, and a host of prescription drugs as well.

Obviously a marijuana cigarette smoked a year ago will not be detectable in a urine test taken today. But it is not possible to be specific about what drugs can be detected by what test over how long a period. There are too many different kinds of drugs and too many different kinds of tests, and the technology of testing is always changing.

A few general observations can be made. The presence of drugs like cocaine and marijuana—the most commonly used substances among teens, can be detected anywhere from a few hours to several weeks after use. Marijuana is detectable longer than cocaine. Therefore, if a person knew that a drug test was to be given on a certain day—let's say opening day of school—then avoiding drugs for a couple of weeks before the test would probably ensure a negative result—no trace of drugs would be found. After the test you could use all the drugs you wanted, unless of course tests were to be conducted regularly every few weeks. That's unlikely. Mass testing is expensive and disruptive. So unannounced testing sweeps like the one described in the opening of this chapter would be the most effective way of using mass screening in schools.

There is a great deal of dispute over how accurate drug tests are. It's fair to say that the more complex and expensive the test the more accurate it is likely to be. Mass screening procedures—testing everybody in your high school—would probably be carried out with less complex and less expensive tests. Some of the best tests cost forty, fifty, or even a hundred dollars each. Multiply that by the number of students in your school, and you will see that state-of-the-art drug testing will quickly eat up a considerable portion of the school budget. Tests for under ten dollars are available—but these tests are responsible for a lot of mistakes.

No test is 100-percent perfect. The better tests claim around 95-percent accuracy. That sounds pretty good. But what it really means is that in one in twenty tests you get the wrong answer. Sometimes the error will be a false negative—drugs are incorrectly not detected in the sample. Other errors will be false positives—the test will say that drugs are present when they are not. There are lots of technical reasons why both false negatives and false positives occur. There is no way to eliminate mistakes completely. How would you like to be one of those whose test showed up as a false positive?

Most suggestions for mass testing of students include a provision that a positive result on the first test be followed up by a second and more sensitive test. Even if that second test showed up negative, do you think everyone would forget that first result? Wouldn't a cloud of suspicion continue to hang over you? We certainly think it would. Besides, follow-up tests are time-consuming and expensive.

Exact figures on test accuracy are hard to come by. Most of the information is issued by the companies that manufacture the test, or the laboratories that administer them. It's in the interest of these groups to make the tests sound as accurate as possible. Yet it has been estimated that the most commonly used urinalysis test may give false positives anywhere from 10 to 30 percent of the time. In mass screening that would mean a huge number of errors. Aside from the technical problems with tests that inevitably produce incorrect results, there are even more serious problems with human error.

The Boxer's Test

Here is an example of how human error can make a test go wrong. Late in 1986 boxer Tim Witherspoon was knocked out in the first round by James "Bonecrusher" Smith. Witherspoon had been expected to win, and his performance was so terrible a lot of people at ringside assumed that something was wrong with him.

Drug tests are part of the regular examination after every fight in New York State, where the fight was held. Witherspoon's urine revealed traces of marijuana. The fighter was about to be suspended. Witherspoon protested. "I was shocked," he said. "I didn't smoke marijuana." But the test results, coupled with his poor performance in the ring, weighed heavily against him. Most people assumed that Tim Witherspoon had indeed smoked marijuana and that somehow that had affected his ability to fight. The story got wide publicity.

A couple of days after the test results were announced, the chairman of the New York State Athletic Commission called Tim Witherspoon to apologize. Somebody in the office had misread the label on the specimen bottle. It was said the commissioner called it a "clerical error." The commissioner made his apology and explanation public, and the fighter's license and reputation were saved. But what if the clerical error had not been detected? What if the victim of the error had not been a well-known fighter, but some unknown high school athlete?

A single, highly trained laboratory worker testing a single urine sample is not likely to make a clerical or other sort of error. But with mass testing, thousands of specimens are going to be processed by relatively untrained poorly paid lab technicians. The work is extremely boring, and mistakes will be made. That is inevitable.

Information on how well testing labs do their job is even

harder to obtain than information on the accuracy of the tests themselves. But from time to time investigations have indicated that a lot of mistakes are made by laboratories, not only with drug tests but with all sorts of medical tests.

Right now the drug-testing business is booming. But the more tests that are given, the more poorly trained, bored, and careless employees will be handling the results—and the greater the chance of error.

Even some in the testing industry are worried about explosive growth. One company director quoted in *The Washington Post* said, "Right now, a lot of labs are cropping up claiming they can do drug testing when, in fact, they cannot."

The business of established drug-testing companies has gone up anywhere from 300 to 400 percent over the last few years. One of the best-selling test items is a kit called "Aware" that parents can use on their own children! It costs $24.95 and includes a specimen bottle, a disclosure form, and a mailing label. Parents can collect a urine sample and mail it to the company, where it will be tested for marijuana, cocaine, PCP, barbiturates, and Valium.

The president of the company was quoted in *The Washington Post* as saying, "I can't even count the calls the [company] got from parents saying, 'I want to know if my kids are using drugs—I'm scared to death.' " The company hoped to sell over 100,000 "Aware" kits in the first year.

How About Rights?

While even the most enthusiastic proponents of mass drug screening will admit that the tests can produce the wrong results some of the time, they say that this fear is exaggerated and that the errors can be virtually eliminated by more sensitive follow-up tests. But in the end the argument is that the potential value of such tests far outweighs the small chance of possible error.

The second major argument against mass drug testing of high school students is that such testing is simply unconstitutional. The Founding Fathers of our country were very concerned about invasions of their privacy. In Colonial America the agents of King George were able to search anyone and see if they were violating the Stamp Act or committing other offenses against the Crown. The enormous resentment caused by these intrusions was one of the causes of the American Revolution.

So when the Founding Fathers sat down to draw up a Constitution for the new United States they were very careful about protecting citizens against the sort of government intrusions they had so hated under the British. On the other hand the Founding Fathers realized that government authorities, such as police, must have the ability to search a person if they believe the person has committed a crime, or has evidence of a crime. The balance between these two needs is found in the Fourth Amendment of the Constitution. The Fourth Amendment protects the individual against being searched unless the police or other authorities have a good reason to believe that a person has evidence of a crime. But you can't search everyone, innocent and guilty, just to find the few who are guilty. Forcing everyone in a high school to take a test for drugs just to find the few who may actually be using them would seem to be clearly unconstitutional.

Yet there is a lot of mass drug testing that goes on in our society. Many companies require drug tests from employees before they can be hired. But companies are not the government, and they are not high schools. If you don't want to take a drug test you don't have to take the job. You have to go to school, and if the school you go to requires drug tests, then you have to take a drug test.

Some school districts have claimed that testing students for drugs does not violate the Fourth Amendment. In 1985 the Board of Education at Becton Regional High School in New Jersey voted to require drug tests for all students. The school superintendent argued that drug taking was basically a health problem, and that the test, which was to be given as part of a comprehensive physical examination, was really not a violation of a student's constitutional rights. The superintendent, Alfred L. Marbaise, said:

"If someone is ingesting into their system some illegal substance, does that give that person the right to begin to destroy themselves and in essence start destroying their own family and destroying other people around them? I concur with the American Medical Association and the World Health Organization, we're dealing with a disease. Alcoholism and narcotics addictions are diseases. We have to treat them as diseases. First of all, they have to be identified. And how do you identify them?"

A lot of people agreed with the superintendent, but there were objections to the policy as well, and it was brought to court. The first legal rulings went against the school board. The court held that the proposed tests did indeed violate the students' constitutional protections against invasion of privacy and unreasonable search and seizure. The court rejected the notion that drug tests were simply another medical test.

But the case is not over. Court decisions can always be appealed to a higher court, and decisions are often reversed. Other school districts may come up with other plans for drug testing. Courts may view different plans more favorably than they did the Becton plan. Over the last few years court decisions have been running against mandatory drug testing, not only in schools but elsewhere. Only a handful of public school districts have even attempted to formulate mass screening plans so far, though there is a lot of interest.

Individual Rights vs. Group Rights

One of the major arguments raised in favor of mass drug testing of students is that illegal drug use harms not only the student who is taking the drugs, but all those with whom he or she comes in contact. Says Superintendent Marbaise: "... When they [the drug users] come into school under the influence, they are beginning to violate the rights of every other student and every other person in the school system...."

Certainly if a student is coming to class stoned every day and falls asleep, begins acting bizarrely, or worse, is dealing drugs in the halls, then more than individual rights are involved. However, if a student's behavior is such that school officials can reasonably conclude that a particular individual may be on drugs, then a drug test can be ordered. But that is very different from requiring everyone in school to take a test. Drug tests might even be ordered for a student whose grades suddenly drop off for no apparent reason, or who begins skipping school. Once again there is some reason to suspect that drugs are being taken.

What if you do smoke a few joints, or snort some cocaine on weekends? If you don't do it in school, and the occasional use of drugs does not affect your school work, is it any of the school's business what you do in your free time?

We've talked to a number of top students who are also occasional drug users. They feel very strongly that what they do outside of school is their own business. We pointed out that drug taking, even if they felt it was not harmful to them, is still an illegal activity. So is drinking, they said. So is driving too fast. Both these activities, they insist, are far more dangerous than occasional drug use—and statistics back up this argument. Yet most schools do not feel compelled to monitor weekend drinking or a student's speeding tickets. These teens were outraged at the unfairness of it all.

Their arguments make sense, but good sense is in short supply in the current drug controversy. There is an enormous amount of emotion surrounding the subject of teens and drugs. If you're caught using drugs, don't expect arguments, no matter how sound they may be, to carry much weight. You are almost certainly going to be in serious trouble.

The Real Reason for Testing

When you examine the case advanced for mass drug testing of high school students it doesn't take long to discover the real reason behind most of the arguments. The tests are to be used as a means of scaring students—you—into not taking drugs.

And that might work. Let's say that like so many teens you are an occasional marijuana smoker. You don't think there is anything wrong with it. You enjoy smoking, but you can take it or leave it. Then one day your school begins a drug screening policy—everybody has to take a urine test.

Would that policy make you give up the marijuana—at least during the school year? You might resent the tests and grumble about an invasion of privacy. But you'd probably stop the pot—because the pleasure it gave you would not be worth the trouble you could get into if your urine test was reported positive for drugs. Most tests are not sensitive enough to tell the difference between the occasional user and the heavy user.

Would the threat of a drug test stop someone with a serious drug problem—the kid who was dependent on or even addicted to drugs? Probably not. He would find a way to beat the test—a kid who is clever enough to successfully hide a serious drug problem may well be clever enough to find a way to fool the drug test. Or he might simply drop out of school to avoid taking the test.

If drug taking was detected, what then? The student might be suspended from school. He might lose his driver's license. Some sort of treatment or counseling would be advised or required. His parents would certainly be told, and the police might also be notified. He might be questioned as to who supplied the drugs. He could be pressured to incriminate his friends who are also using drugs.

Those are fairly severe penalties. And the threat might well shock the occasional user into becoming a nonuser. But will these penalties change the behavior of the heavy user—the kid who is really in trouble? Maybe, but somehow we doubt it. The habitual user is already running serious risks—and knows it. He can't stop, that's his problem.

There aren't really enough counseling and treatment programs for the drug users that we know about now. There is no indication that the government or anyone else is going to spend a lot more money establishing new programs. And in the end there are some serious questions as to just how effective most counseling and treatment programs are for heavy drug users. So just to say the drug user will be sent to "treatment or counseling," without really looking at the effectiveness of the program, and who is going to pay for it, is not realistic or honest.

Another argument that is frequently used in favor of mass

screening is that it will produce a "drug-free school." What that really means is all the kids who are caught using drugs will be thrown out. That may make some school administrators feel good, but kids who use drugs are not going to disappear completely. They will still be out there, on the street corner or at the mall. If you had a friend who was kicked out of school for using drugs, he's still going to be your friend. You may not see him in class, but you can still see him every day if you wish. You might even find him more attractive, because you feel that he has been wronged by an adult society that doesn't understand him —or you.

Finally, those who argue in favor of mass drug screening insist that it helps to establish a social climate in which drug use simply will not be permitted or tolerated—no matter what the cost.

Mass drug screening is certainly evidence of a tough antidrug stand. But there has never been a time when drug use among high school students has been officially tolerated. Schools are always being swept by changing fashions in antidrug programs. Some programs emphasize a "soft" educational approach, others a tough "test everyone" approach—and all shades in between. There is very little hard evidence to suggest that one approach is any better than another.

As should be fairly obvious by now, we do not favor mass drug testing of high school students. We don't think it would be effective, and it could lead to some real injustices when the tests come out wrong—and some of them would. The threat of drug tests might scare off some of the casual users, but unless you are one of those who believes that occasional use inevitably leads to addiction, it's the casual user who doesn't have the problem. The heavy user or the addict isn't going to be scared off by the threat of a test. In fact, many may be worse off by being forced out of school and into the streets.

The testing issue is being exploited. The test manufacturers and laboratories are naturally pushing mass testing. It's going to mean big bucks for them. There are some politicians who are trying to ride the issue for their own advantage. Drug testing makes an easy slogan. If you're against testing that means you're soft on drugs—and no one wants to be labeled as being "soft on drugs." Once the testing gets into politics it's hard to argue against. Right now testing of one sort or another is being promoted as the solution to a lot of problems. Give people lie-detector tests, or AIDS tests, or drug tests, and these problems will be solved somehow.

But most people who support mass testing are not trying to exploit the issue. They're scared and they just don't know what else to do. Parents—maybe your parents—have heard about the drug "epidemic" among teens. Even if they don't think you're on drugs, they worry about the kids you hang around with—they worry about "peer pressure." If drugs are everywhere in your school, won't you somehow be led or pressured into taking them? They love you. They want to protect you.

To most parents the specter of a teenage drug "epidemic" is a very immediate problem. They see your life and future in peril. The guarantees of the Constitution about unreasonable search and seizure seem remote. Stopping kids from using drugs outweighs everything else.

That's an understandable reaction, but a panicky one that sends the wrong message. The Constitution should mean something, even if you still happen to be in school. If mass drug screening in schools ever becomes common, if the scene that we described at the beginning of this chapter moves from imagination to reality, then schools are going to feel a lot more like prison camps than they do now. No one will gain from that.

In the end we believe that we must rely on the strength of our society, not on our fears, not on our suspicions. We're a free society. Freedom has its dangers—because sometimes people are going to do things that are not good for society, and not good for the individual. Even with its dangers freedom is a lot better than the alternative. We can't rely on tests or any other scheme to trap or terrify people into good behavior. In the end it's really up to you.

11

Highs Without Drugs

Ever watch a little kid on a swing? Or watch a kid spinning round and round enjoying getting dizzy? Swinging, spinning, bouncing up and down on a pogo stick, these are playful, mood-altering activities. But you don't have to be a little kid to get high without drugs.

Sure, drugs are a fast, easy route to a high. If they weren't, who would take them? But the choice in life is not between taking drugs and missing out on all the fun.

Consider the surge of euphoria you feel on a plummeting roller coaster. Amusement park rides simulate many of the effects of drugs. Go to an amusement park with a bunch of friends and you'll probably laugh your way through being banged up, shaken up, and thrown around. Amusement parks are a psychoactive experience.

And what can LSD make you see that Steven Spielberg can't? Exciting movies with dazzling special effects provide quite a jolt. So can escapist fiction. Anything from a romance novel to a Stephen King tale of horror can be totally absorbing, depending on what you like to read. If you're a sci-fi fan, reading science fiction will energize your imagination. Music can energize, too, and music can also relax and soothe.

Sports may be the greatest nondrug high of all. We're not just talking about sports as a physical activity for athletes. We mean spectator sports, too. Ever been in a stadium rooting for your team along with thousands of other fans? Depending on your team's success or failure your mood shifts from wild high to dejected low. Sports really get the adrenaline flowing.

The high you get from drugs is really a passive high. It comes completely from without. The high you get when you sing in your high school musical, dance in a recital, or act in a play comes from within. You have created the stimulation and excitement. You're an active participant in your own adventure. The applause you get from the audience gives you quite a lift.

Sometimes life tosses us a high when we least expect it. Getting an *A* on a test you thought you'd get a *C* on, finding out the girl or boy you secretly like likes you too, winning the school popularity contest, making the team, being chosen editor of the yearbook, or getting into the college of your dreams will change a down mood to an up mood instantly.

But wait a minute. What about the other side of that? On the low days when everything's gone wrong, what besides drugs will make you feel better? Only the passage of time, making changes in your life, seeking help, and learning to handle disappointments.

We know those aren't easy answers but there's just no quick fix to life. There's no such thing as an eternal high. Even the brightest, best looking, and most popular teenagers run into lows. Everybody gets hurt, everybody feels pain, everybody loses sometimes. A big part of growing up is developing the strength and self-knowledge to handle lows. It's something you can't get through drugs.

12

Some Things to Remember

Drugs

• The word *drug* is a broad one. Aspirin and penicillin are drugs. But when people talk about drug abuse and drug raids, those are not the sorts of drugs they are talking about.

• The drug in *drug abuse* is practically any substance that alters your mood or changes your perception, that gives you a thrill, wakes you up, calms you down, puts you to sleep, or simply keeps you from feeling worse. In practical terms a drug is a socially disapproved or illegal substance that changes your mood or perception.

• Any drug or substance can be abused.

• In America, indeed in the Western world, alcohol is and always has been the drug of choice. It is enjoyed by a majority of the population and has created terrible problems for a minority. It's legal, though probably not for you. If you are caught as an underage drinker you may have some problems. If you are caught using other kinds of drugs you are going to have much bigger problems.

• Both caffeine in coffee and nicotine in tobacco products should be considered drugs. Both are addictive, and nicotine is one of the most addictive drugs in use. Both are quite legal.

• The products of the opium poppy are among the most ancient and widely used drugs. In one form or another opium has been "eaten," or more accurately drunk, smoked, sniffed, and injected for centuries.

• The most notorious drug used in America today is heroin. Heroin is highly addictive—addiction can occur within a few weeks. Heroin addiction has proved to be extremely difficult to break.

• Heroin is also injected intravenously—directly into the vein. Along with all of the other problems associated with intravenous drug use, a new terror has been added, the deadly disease AIDS. AIDS is spreading most rapidly among IV drug users, because of needle sharing.

• The leaves of the coca plant, which contain cocaine, are chewed by some of the Indians of South America in order to fight off fatigue, cold, and hunger.

• Cocaine has had an up-and-down history in the U.S. and Europe. During the last century it was used as an anesthetic, and for other strictly medicinal purposes. It was also popular as a recreational drug and was found in a variety of tonics and patent medicines.

• Cocaine in powdered form that could be inhaled or snorted became the high-priced glamor drug of the eighties. By the late eighties a freebase, smokable form of cocaine commonly called crack, was widely available at a price that made it attractive to the poor.

• Cocaine is a stimulant, and while it is primarily used for its pleasurable effects, some athletes have used it to improve performance.

• While cocaine is not nearly as physically addictive as heroin, it is an easy drug to become dependent upon. After the short-lived jolt of energy and rush of good feeling there is a down period, and many users are tempted to take more of the drug to get over the bad feelings.

• The line between physical addiction and psychological dependence is sometimes a hard one to draw.

• Chronic overuse of cocaine tends to lead to insomnia, irritability, paranoid feelings, and in rare cases psychotic episodes. Snorting cocaine also irritates the nose.

• There is some evidence, or at least suspicion, that cocaine can interfere with the electrical activity of the heart—and in rare cases bring on a fatal seizure.

• Marijuana (cannabis) is another ancient and widely used substance, but should not be lumped into the same category as heroin or cocaine.

• For most the occasional joint is no more dangerous than the occasional beer. A couple of beers can be dangerous if you are driving. So can a couple of joints.

• While not addicting, marijuana can be habit-forming. There is no evidence, however, that marijuana use inevitably or even frequently leads to the use of harder drugs.

• If your parents find you sneaking a few beers it may upset them. If they find you smoking pot it will probably scare the hell out of them.

• There is no solid evidence that there are any particular ill effects from long-term, occasional marijuana use. But taking smoke into your lungs, from tobacco or marijuana, can't be good for you. There is some evidence to suggest that long-term heavy use can have serious health effects.

• If you want to know what addiction or drug dependence is like, watch a heavy smoker trying to give up cigarettes.

• Adult panic over glue sniffing is an unnecessary overreaction. Glue sniffing is a foolish and childish activity, more likely to make you sick than high. Kids get over it. There are no adult glue addicts.

• Barbiturates and tranquilizers have been used medically

as sedatives and sleeping pills. As street drugs called downers, they have been used to produce an alcohol-like, drunken state.

• The greatest immediate danger from downers is an overdose that will put you to sleep permanently. Tranquilizers and sleeping pills are frequently used in suicide attempts—all too often successful ones.

• Mixing drugs—any kind of drugs—is dangerous. Mixing downers with alcohol is exceptionally dangerous.

• Amphetamines are synthetic stimulants. Throughout the fifties and sixties they were widely prescribed, and probably overprescribed, to ease fatigue, depression, and to help curb the appetite and lose weight.

• Amphetamines have been used legally and illegally by long-distance truckers, athletes, dancers, and actors, and often students who needed to stay awake for long periods of studying.

• The most dangerous form of amphetamine is speed that is injected intravenously and produces an immediate and powerful jolt or rush of energy.

• The psychedelic or hallucinogenic drugs, notably LSD, are among the most praised and damned drugs of modern times. There is no evidence that LSD damages the brain, the chromosomes, or does any other physical harm. On the other hand there is also no evidence that the drug makes one more creative, insightful, or happier either.

• The psychedelic drugs can provide a powerful experience or trip that can be very pleasant or horrifyingly bad—depending on the circumstances. If taken at all the drugs must be used in a relaxed and pleasant setting, while surrounded by understanding friends.

• Ultimately many LSD users find the experience repetitive.

• There is some evidence that the LSD experience, like any

other strong experience, may trigger psychotic episodes in individuals whose mental balance is already delicate.

• Anabolic steroids, or synthetic male hormones, do increase muscles, and probably enhance strength and athletic performance.

• Steroids tend to make users feel bloated and sluggish.

• Steriods are extremely powerful drugs that upset the body's delicate hormone balance. The long-term effects of steroid use are not fully known, but the potential damage looks very scary indeed.

• Any drug can be dangerous during pregnancy.

The Law

• Since 1914 most opium products and cocaine have been illegal in the United States.

• Marijuana has been essentially illegal since 1934.

• The aim of all the laws has been to produce a drug-free society. The laws have not worked; serious drug abuse appears to be at about the same level it always was.

• Restrictive laws have made addicts criminals, because they are dependent on an illegal substance, and because they often have to commit crimes to support their habit.

• Like the prohibition of alcohol, the prohibition of drugs has led to the creation of a vast, powerful, and violent criminal network that, despite one war on drugs after another, the authorities seem quite powerless to curb.

• Local laws and attitudes about the possession and use of small quantities of drugs, particularly marijuana, vary a good deal from time to time and place to place. Sometimes use is legally winked at. Other times it is treated more severely than many violent crimes.

• Everyone acknowledges that the laws regarding drugs have not been effective, and have often been counterproductive. No one has the faintest notion of what to do about them.

• Modest suggestions about the decriminalization of marijuana, or supplying free clean needles to heroin addicts so they can avoid AIDS, have been met with howls of outrage.

• Illogical, ineffective, and hypocritical as they may be, there is absolutely no reason to believe that the drug laws will be changed in any meaningful way. We're all going to have to live with them.

Society

• Every society, with the exception of the Eskimos, who couldn't get them, has used drugs.

• The fear created by drug use—particularly drug use among teens—is out of proportion to the actual problem. That's not going to change either.

• Drugs have had their most devastating effect upon the poor, particularly the black and Hispanic inner-city poor.

• Publicly funded treatment centers for the truly addicted are totally inadequate.

• For reasons that no one fully understands, drug use overall ebbs and flows, and there are changes in drug fashions. Recently marijuana use has dropped, cocaine use has risen.

• There appears to be a particular subgroup in our society —and probably most societies—who are going to become seriously drug-dependent no matter what. The more medical attention they receive, and the less political attention, the better for all of us.

Testing

• Drugs use can be detected by a variety of blood and particularly urine tests. But the sensitivity of these tests varies greatly, as does the cost.

• The most commonly used of these tests are pretty good

at detecting marijuana use, even after several weeks. They are also good at detecting heroin or other narcotics that are not widely used. They are not good at all for detecting cocaine or alcohol.

• No test is perfect, and mistakes in urinalysis drug tests are quite common, particularly in inexpensive mass tests.

• Mass drug screening of high school students has been proposed but there are serious doubts whether such measures would be constitutional. Recently most court decisions have gone against mass testing, but the issue has not been finally and definitively resolved.

• Private employers and private schools can and sometimes do require testing of all employees or students.

• If the authorities—police, school, whatever—have reason to suspect that an individual has been using illegal drugs, it is then legal to order a drug test.

Drugs and You

• The best possible advice we can give about illegal drugs is don't use 'em. The really powerful ones like heroin are dangerously addictive. The milder drugs like marijuana aren't worth the effort.

• While it is possible to state what the general effect of a drug will be, reactions are very individualized. A drug that one person may find pleasantly stimulating can make another feel jumpy, irritable, depressed, or paranoid.

• Some people can take drugs, even those known to be addicting, without becoming addicted or dependent. Others succumb quickly, either physically or psychologically. There is, unfortunately, no foolproof way of predicting which sort of person you are. Like so much else about taking drugs today, it has an element of Russian roulette.

• If you are using any drug regularly, just to help you get through the day, you're in trouble.

• If you use drugs you probably get them from your friends, but somewhere along the line someone is doing business with professional drug dealers.

• If you use street drugs you can never be sure what you are really getting, therefore you can never predict how the drug will affect you.

• History has shown that neither preaching, nor education, nor the police are going to keep drugs out of the hands of those who want them. We do not live in a drug-free society, and are not likely to. The ultimate decision about drug use is going to be up to you. Make it wisely. You can get high without them.

13

If You Need Help

As we said, the best way to handle drugs in today's world is to stay away from them. They simply are not worth the problems they can create.

However, we are realistic enough to know that we do not live in a drug-free society—and we probably never will. You're going to confront some drugs in your life, and if statistics are accurate the chances are fifty-fifty that you've already tried some. For most teens, now as before, drugs will be a minor part of your life. Many of the pot smokers and acid droppers of the sixties are now parents worrying about their own kids. But not everyone passes through the drug experience unscathed. There are those for whom drugs can be a problem—sometimes a very big problem. There is no way of predicting who is going to have the problem.

When we say problem we don't just mean the heroin addict breaking into homes to support a $300-a-day habit. It's obvious that he's *got* a problem, and that he *is* a problem. We're talking about the kid who needs something to get through the day, to confront the ordinary everyday stresses and tensions, and the sometimes crushing boredom of the teen years. We're talking about the kid who finds drugs occupying an ever larger part of his or her time and attention.

If that's you, then you've got a problem. You'd better do something about it, because if you don't the consequences can be severe—physically, emotionally, and legally.

Usually talking to your friends is a good idea, but with drugs it may not be. If your friends are also doing drugs they won't be much help. If your friends are completely off drugs, then their reaction might be so negative, so moralistic, that you won't want to listen.

It would be great if you could talk to your parents. But we realize that drugs are even tougher to talk about with parents than sex—and sex is tough enough. But if you feel you do have good rapport with your parents, and that if they can't understand what you're going through they will at least be sympathetic, will not become hysterical, and not lean on you too hard—then that is by far the best place to start. If not your parents then an uncle, aunt, cousin, any older relative you are close to should help.

Failing that you might try a school guidance counselor or school psychologist, if you have someone you like and trust. There are also clergymen and doctors—some of them surprisingly understanding and knowledgeable.

You can go to your local phone book and look under "Drug Abuse and Treatment," or some such heading, and you'll probably find several places listed. Be very careful here. All sorts of centers, clinics, and therapists may be listed—and there is no easy way of telling how good or bad one may be. The profit-making centers can be extremely expensive, and they have a vested interest in getting you into their form of treatment. They may have their own profits, rather than your best interests, at heart. Some therapists are excellent, others are complete quacks. Unless you have strong recommendations, try to stick to the centers that are publicly funded, though waiting lists are often long.

You may also find listings for local drug hotlines that you can call in your area. Sometimes these hotlines are listed in the front of the phone book along with the police and fire departments.

There are a couple of national numbers you can call too:

The National Drug Hotline
1–800–662–HELP (1–800–662–4357)
The Cocaine Hotline
1–800–COCAINE (1–800–262–2463)

Both of these lines are open till the wee hours of the morning, and a sympathetic and knowledgeable person will give you immediate advice and try to refer you to help in your area. A word of warning—these lines, particularly the Cocaine Hotline, tend to be very busy. Be persistent, keep trying.

You can call various service or charitable organizations not directly or exclusively concerned with drugs, like the Big Brothers and Big Sisters, The United Way, even Alcoholics Anonymous. They may be able to point you in the right direction. If you don't have a phone book simply call the operator and explain what you want. Most are very helpful.

If you feel totally overwhelmed, and in immediate physical peril, there is always the emergency ward of the nearest hospital. Emergency wards are not really structured to handle emotional problems—but they may be better than nothing. Really large hospitals may also have walk-in psychiatric services.

There are several self-help groups for drug abusers that are based on the philosophy of Alcoholics Anonymous.

Narcotics Anonymous World Service Office, Inc.
P. O. Box 9999
Van Nuys, CA 91490

Cocaine Anonymous
335 North La Brea Ave.
Los Angeles, CA 90036

If you have to do a report on drugs and drug abuse a good source for information is:

The National Institute of Drug Abuse
P. O. Box 2345
Rockville, MD 20850

Books and Films

There are enormous numbers of books that have been written on the subject of drugs. A quick check of *Books in Print* in your local library will provide a staggering and daunting list. For the general reader most of these books are too technical, out of date, badly biased, or just plain bad. What we have provided is a small, representative sampling of books that you might find interesting and useful. A couple of them are novels.

The explosive growth of the use of the VCR has changed the way we view films. Now old films, which may have shown up only rarely on television, if at all, can be seen. So we have also included a short list of films about drugs or drug users.

Books

Abel, Ernest. *Marihuana: The First Twelve Thousand Years.* London: Plenum Press, 1980. More about cannabis than you really need or want to know.

Brecher, Edward M., and the editors of *Consumer Reports.*

Licit and Illicit Drugs. Boston: Little, Brown, 1974. Though now a bit dated, this book remains one of the best and most intelligent overviews of drug use in America.

Goldman, Bob, with Bush, Patricia, and Klatz, Ronald. *Death in the Locker Room: Steroids and Cocaine in Sports* (revised). Tucson, Ariz.: The Body Press, 1987. Really this is a book about steroids, and one of the few available. A bit of information on cocaine was tossed into a new edition to capitalize on the current interest.

Guiles, Fred. *Legend: The Life and Death of Marilyn Monroe.* New York: Stein and Day, 1984. There has been idle speculation that Marilyn was murdered by everyone from the Mafia to the CIA. It is almost certain that she died from an overdose of sleeping pills—probably deliberate.

Hawley, Richard A. *A School Answers Back: Responding to Student Drug Use.* New York: The American Council for Drug Education, 1984. An educator explains his hard-line approach to student drug use.

Hyde, Margaret O. *Mind Drugs.* New York: McGraw-Hill, 1974. Dated, but still a good introduction to the subject for junior high school students.

Meyer, Nicholas. *The Seven-Percent Solution.* New York: Dutton, 1974. A clever pastiche in which a cocaine-addicted Sherlock Holmes meets Dr. Sigmund Freud, who cures him. Also made into an entertaining film.

Newman, Susan. *You Can Say No to a Drink or Drug.* New York: Putnam, 1986. An illustrated guide for teens and pre-teens on how to resist or get out of difficult alcohol and drug-related situations.

Russell, George K. *Marihuana Today* (rev. edition). New York: The Myrin Institute, 1980. A strongly antimarijuana book.

Stafford, Peter. *Psychedelics Encyclopedia.* Los Angeles:

J. P. Tarcher, 1982. Everything you ever wanted to know about psychedelic drugs, and more.

Susann, Jacqueline. *The Valley of the Dolls.* New York: Bantam, 1967. A trashy but extremely popular novel about the use of drugs, particularly downers, among Hollywood's rich and famous. Made into a trashy but extremely popular film.

Weil, Andrew, and Rose, Winifred. *Chocolate to Morphine.* Boston: Houghton Mifflin, 1983. An interesting and well-illustrated overview of drugs. The authors are generally sympathetic to drugs you can grow and chew.

Woodward, Bob. *Wired.* New York: Simon and Schuster, 1984. Subtitled "The short life and fast times of John Belushi," this fascinating and often scary book chronicles the drug use and drug death of the popular comic.

Films

Easy Rider (1969). Directed by Dennis Hopper. With Peter Fonda and Jack Nicholson. This was the quintessential sixties film, with drugs, motorcycles, and the search for the "real" America.

I'm Dancing as Fast As I Can (1982). Directed by Jack Hofsiss. With Jill Clayburgh. Based on Barbara Gordon's true and terrible story of her Valium addiction.

Lenny (1974). Directed by Bob Fosse. With Dustin Hoffman. A shattering film biography of the controversial fifties comic, who died of a drug overdose.

Long Day's Journey into Night (1962). Directed by Sidney Lumet. With Katharine Hepburn and Ralph Richardson. An excellent film adaptation of the Eugene O'Neill autobiographical play. The central figure is the playwright's tragic, morphine-addicted mother.

North Dallas Forty (1974). Directed by Ted Kotcheff. With Nick Nolte. A seriocomic look at life in the NFL. Drug use is a central theme.

Reefer Madness (1936). Directed by Louis Gasnier. With Dave O'Brien and Dorothy Short. A low-budget "warning" film that tells in a hysterical (now hilarious) fashion how a puff of pot can lead clean-cut teenagers to insanity and death. Now a cult classic, often watched by pot smokers. The fate of this film should serve as a warning for all who try to warn kids off drugs by exaggerating the dangers.

Richard Pryor Live on the Sunset Strip (1982). Directed by Joe Layton. This concert film contains Pryor's monologue on his addiction to freebase cocaine. It's funny and so frightening it should scare anyone away from the stuff.

Sid and Nancy (1986). Directed by Alex Cox. With Gary Oldman. The short, drug-centered life and death of British punk rocker Sid Vicious and his strange, mad American girlfriend. What could have been sensationalized or simply bizarre has been made into an affecting and human film.

Up In Smoke (1978). Directed by Lou Adler. With Richard "Cheech" Marin and Thomas Chong. The first of Cheech and Chong's "pothead" comedies. It's stupid but cheerful and funny. It was made at a time when marijuana was still considered funny. It probably wouldn't be made today. W. C. Fields couldn't make his drunk films today either— but they're still funny, too.

Index

162

Index

Athletes (*Cont.*)
  competitiveness, 99
  and drugs, 43–44, 100–101
  Soviet Union, 98
  and steroids, 94
  women, 104
Atlas, Charles, 103

Bach, Johann Sebastian, 80
Balzac, Honoré de, 80
Barbiturates, 83–85, 147–148
  effects, 84
  withdrawal, 83–84
Becton Regional High School, 136
Benzedrine, 87
Bhang, 59
Bias, Len, 44
Black, J.R., 113
Bodybuilders, 103–105
Breathalyzer test, 130

Caffeine, 5, 78–80
Cannabis sativa, 58, 61–62
Chinese (and opium), 20–21
Chloroform, 81
Cigarettes, 6, 41, 145–146
Club de Hachichins, 61
Coca, 35–38
Coca-Cola, 36
Coca leaves, 37–38

Cocaine, 121–122, 146–147
  and athletes, 42–43
  deaths, 44–45
  dependency, 40–42
  effects, 39–42
  as medicine, 38–39
  nineteenth century, 35–36
  origins, 36–37
  regulated, 115–116
Codeine, 9, 23
Coffee, 5, 78–80
Coleridge, Samuel Taylor, 26
Confessions of an English Opium Eater, 25
Cough medicine, 9
Crack, 35, 122, 146
Craving, 22
Crystal, Billy, 94

Death in the Locker Room, 107–108
Demerol, 23
Dentistry (and drugs), 25–26, 81
Dependency, 11, 147
  amphetamines, 88
  cocaine, 40–42
  steroids, 106
  tranquilizers, 86, 87
Depressants, 21–22
De Quincey, Thomas, 25–26